Why Am I Stuck?

The science of releasing yourself from being held a mental hostage

by

Ehryck F. Gilmore, CH

Eromlig Publishing
Chicago, IL

An Eromlig Publishing book published by
arrangement with Ehryck F. Gilmore, CH

ISBN: 0-9759120-3

Edited by Christine Meister, Lissa Woodson and Lynda Byrd
Cover design and logo by Behe-Jahe Williams
Graphics by Douglas Mau

Acclaim for *Why Am I Stuck?*

"People across the nation are talking about Ehryck Gilmore because of his intuitiveness, candor and insightful interpretation of what motivates us all. His unique and honest perspective on how to navigate through life will be talked about for years to come."

Valerie Norman-Gammon,
President & CEO Amethyst Entertainment, Inc.

"Finally, a practical method to finding the courage to design your own life and free yourself from being a mental hostage! Once you have finished this book and apply the principles, your life will never be the same. You will no longer be *stuck* because you will take the first step in pursuing lifelong dreams and desires that have been suppressed due to fear and lack of direction. Reading this book will be an awakening that will result in achieving the impossible and enjoying the full, abundant life that awaits you."

Cheryl Burton, TV News Anchor

"Why Am I Stuck" is an extraordinary "journey" of self-examination that empowers you to get exactly what you want out of life. Learn how your beliefs influence all positive and negative experiences you encounter in your life. "Why Am I Stuck" compels you to dare to dream in a way that is startling, inspirational, instructional and unpredictably humorous!"

Patricia A. Toney, Entertainment Marketing Consultant

"As a developer and coordinator of many charitable events across the United States, my life had become overwhelming. My inability to relax and enjoy life resulted in an illness, which forced me to take a step back and look at exactly what was going on in my life. *Why Am I Stuck* was a guide to feeling fearless and secure and getting a handle on every area of my life. Today, I am proud to say that I now have a better outlook and appreciate the fullness of what life has to offer. I am no longer "stuck," and I believe this book will help many others explore their own possibilities."

Bonnie Fortunato, Vice President & Entrepreneur

Acknowledgments

I am grateful to the Universe for the wonderful gifts bestowed upon me.

I would like to thank everyone who has passed through my life, always encouraging me to aspire to higher spiritual levels. I would also like to thank my mother, father, sisters and brothers. To my family: Behe-Jahe and Eula Williams family; the Fulliloves, the Gilmores, the Yarboroughs, the Nixons, the Hookers, Linda Cobb, the Joneses, the Waters, the James, the Walkers and the Worthingtons, Pastor Bertha Gilmore, for the Bibical references.

I would also like thank Valerie Norman-Gammon, for insisting that I have the proper credentials; and to her husband, Parker for allowing her to mentor me. To Cheryl Burton for always going the extra mile for me, to Patricia A. Toney--thanks for always believing in me from the first day we met. To Bonnie Fortunato and To Lissa Woodson (of Macro Publishing Group) for holding my hand (and squeezing it!) through this adventure and making sure this book got to print. To my editor, Christine Meister.

To Jerry and Esther Hicks "Abraham," you're the greatest and I've learned so much from you. David Gershon and Gail Straub of the Empowerment Institute—there are no words to express how I feel. Larry Garrett and staff—thanks for all the support. To the Liedecker Institute, Dr. Will Horton-NFNLP, the School of Spiritual Psychology in Milwaukee, the NLP Institute of Chicago, Christ Universal Temple, the Moody Bible Institute, DePaul University—SNL, Parto Naderi staff, and the Chicagoland NLP study group, Gayle Seminara-Mandel, Dawn Silver D.N. To Douglas Mau, Linda Byrd and Henrietta Byrd for their special input.

Universal Love to my friends and associates: Jennifer Pope, Jean Ricks, Diane Armour, Bill Silas, Renee McCoy, Pamela Renee Smith, Tina Moore, Monique Boyer, Kellee Warren, Yahoshua Joshua, Giorgio Travoto, Juan Lopez, Nannette Frank, Michael Hearn, Nuhzett Sayrun, A. C. McLean; and the following family groups: Valerie Landfair, R &

J. Genus, M. Colston-Davis, B. Gilbert-Turner, Elaine Williams; the Brit-Handys, the Britton-Gibsons, Dr. A. Bailey, Debbie Buie, M&N Balls, Carol Starks, the Violet Clarke and C & R Peppers, Claire Brown-DeBrie & Dennis. Also to Bibba-Biss Boutique, E. Adams, the Wednesday Wicker Park Social Group (you know who you are!); to my Friday and Saturday "current events" group (you know who you are, too!); to Diann Burns, DaVida Rice, Andre Walker, Roosevelt Cartwright, P. McCain, the Jackson-Laurents, Luella Holman (Big thanks for the push!), Terry Prince and A. Craft. Pam Payne, Shevette Williams, Dr. Michael Senegal, Deborah Turner, Barbra Cromartie, Patrice Kennedy; to Mia Walden, R. BallaSaum, Dr. D. Sturgis-Hinton, Dr. G. Jackson, Dr. A. Foggs, Dr. G. Bibbs, Dr. D. Coynik, W. R. Morton, Rochell Potts, R. Dalton, Phyliss Nash, Y. Granberry, D. F. Wesley, M. D. Heard, Sheila Rivera, S. Green-Smith, A. K. Barratt, Dr. Gail Street, G. Ford, Y. Graham, J. Robinson-Brown, T. Battles, Burt Wilson, Roscoe Lacey, Felicia Carr, J. Green-Toney, A. J. Thompson, Karen Weddington, and to Marzett Ahmed-Otis, P. Walker-Thomas, S. Siggal, G. Pope-Wimp, E.Cooper, C.Edgerson, A.White, L.Hand, A.Bundy and Linda Clifford, Louise Arnone and Family.

If I forgot anyone, your name goes here: ______________________________. Please, please, please charge it to my head and not my heart.

Isn't life wonderful? The Universe has brought us all together. Although we are on different paths, we share the fruits of the Universe.

Ehryck F. Gimore, CH

When you cut off the light,
make sure your brain stays on

When I first decided to write this book, I was confident that I could, in the most simplistic terms, explain life's little traumas in a common sense framework. That I could stay on point, but not rehash so much of what already sits on the bookstore shelves. But I wanted a book from a point of view that was not too esoteric. Esoteric in the New Age sense that you had to study with some Guru on a mountaintop to understand it.

I wanted this book to be written so that if you were Esoterically Enlightened you could feel good reading the message again. But if you were a new student to the laws that govern the Universe, or just seeking understanding about what's happening in your life, you could read this book and walk away with a newfound understanding.

It is my hope that ***Why Am I Stuck?*** provides an understanding of the manifestations and wonderful contrasts the Universe offers. Whether it is the good, the bad or the ugly, it's all a part of the Universe.

Within this book you will find suggestions on how to get *unstuck*, and the reasons why one might be stuck in the first place. Each reason tends to build on the other, laying out a blueprint of how one might find themselves entrenched and overwhelmed. I will also encourage you throughout this book to delve deep into your heart, to pull the issues from under your bed which you have conveniently stored away, and help unravel the reasons why you are getting the same results and haven't been able to move forward in life.

At the end of each chapter you will be given a space to record your thoughts about what you have read. While **JOURNALING**, you will be able to document your achievements as you work toward improving your life and obtaining your goals and desires. I suggest that you work with a friend, in this way you will have a partner to monitor your progress. There will be definitions to check to see if the meanings of the words you use now actually matches how you integrate them into your life.

Also there will be a series of short case studies which provides a glimpse into the life of my clients who have applied some of my suggestions as they, too, tried to become unstuck. Clients like Wendy, who is an executive manager in the criminal justice system. Wendy had allowed, what I call the "*As soon as I* (get a new car, buy a new home, secure that next promotion), stand in her way of living in the "Now." All of her happiness was tied to, and based on, some circumstance happening before she could take the next step. Wendy confessed to me that the system had taken its toll on her. Most times she felt as though all of her "pretty balloons" filled with her desires and dreams had the helium stolen from them by the people she tried to help.

Wendy, is like so many others: exceptional in her career but not in her personal life. She had good intentions but was unmotivated and without direction. As I listened to her situation, I finally told her: "you need a script, (a/k/a "Goal") a small one first, then on to a bigger one. Following a script with an ending that parallels her goals and dreams gives her the tools to take some action in brining her closer to her desires.

This is just one story exploring how people from every walk of life—business executives, entertainers, entrepreneurs to 9-to-5 workers react to their current situation. Whether you are a high-powered executive, deciding to make a move toward starting your business, or a housewife who has given up her dreams and desires to take care of her family, you will find solace in these stories.

Explore how each person in the story reacts to their challenges and applies credible advice which they can follow for reaching their goal and desires. Slipping and getting stuck in no way prevents you from finding a solution. I'm not sure how many people know that they have the power to create a life of total bliss right here on Earth. There is so much wealth right here, an abundance of knowledge that is more than anyone could imagine. There is not one library in the whole world that could provide enough space to hold this undiminished vital information. Not everyone will be aware of how vast this Universal supply is and how gifted each person is on his own level. There is not one

who can say that they have not been given the tools of the Universe. People can say that they do not know how to work with them, but they have access to all the tools that were given to them. Call on your higher self to assist you when you can not walk alone. Call on your higher self when you need additional resources. There may be times when you think the Universe is not responding, but that is only because you are not sending out a direct signal. Look in side of your mind to see what your heart truly desires. Look to see what your goals in life are and then allow for Universal manifestation. **"How can I know you, If I can't think about you" ... On to me send me your woes, So says the Universe.** There may be times that you can not see beyond "what is "or what is in front of your face because you have become one with the condition. The condition that you no longer are wanting to be associated with. This is the time to think what would make me whole? what would make me smile again? what would make me one with the Universe. Even-though the sunshines everyday does not mean you will always be in it. But you do know that it does shine everyday some where if you are willing to become one with your dreams, desires, and goals you must stop feeding the energy you now know as comfortable. Two energies cannot occupy the same space, so when you are in a space of discomfort that means there is no energy of Universal love shining in. Allow yourself to be all that you say you are, listen to your words and see if they match up to what your are saying. When you say I'm a good person the word good means you are above the negative, so reflect what you say. The vibrations you offer to the Universe will be reflected back to you. This is how you will reap your good from the Universe. Think of your words in the graphic form of a boomerang, "what is thrown is returned." Every bit of the Universe is designed to make our life happier, vibrant and more f ulfilled. How ever you're not here just to ride. At some point in your life, you must be in the driver's seat!
What will you do when you take the wheel?

Do I know what I want?
Then...

CHAPTER 1
WHY AM I STUCK?

Why am I stuck? The question begs an answer. If you ask people, "*What is it that you want out of life?*" You will find a surprising number can't answer. Even a few moments later they are still staring blankly ahead, their eyes wide with fright—the classic "deer caught in the headlights" look.

One of the reasons they are unable to give you an honest answer could be that they are stuck in the land of OZ or some other fairytale land, searching and searching for the road to clarity?

There are several reasons for being **stuck**. One could be the inability to move forward. Maybe you're afraid of what will happen if you fail. If you falter, where can you place that blame? Condemnation, guilt, criticism and blame by any other name, plays such a huge role in our daily lives. And as a rule, people do not like to place blame on their own shoulders.

Looking in the mirror for answers many times may cause more anguish. Because all you will see is you and no one else.

And that is the point here—questions begin and end with you. Answers begin and end with you.

Maybe you're saying to yourself, "What does this have to do with me?" Or are you saying, "I'm not stuck, I'm just a little off track. As soon as I take care of these outstanding business matters, I'm going to start working on my project again." The bottom line is that people will give all kinds of "reasons" or shall we say—excuses? Things such as, I need to wait for the money to start coming in, I have to wait until the kids to go off to school, or just the plain old story about how you don't have enough time. So when I use the word "stuck" it doesn't mean you have not made any progress toward your goals, it just means you got sidetracked and can't figure out how to mentally reenergize yourself.

Suggestion: Reboot your project. One way you could do this is pull out your old notes and clarify them. Are these goals attainable with your current thought patterns? Another way could be if you compared notes to someone who is working toward a similar desire or goal.

Stuck is a condition we all reach at one time or another in our lives—an imaginary mental state of perpetual standstill. Just like a car lodged in a muddy ditch, the car may rock forward a little or even back a few inches. The wheels turn feverishly but eventually go nowhere. The road that will take the car to its true destination lay only a few feet away from the ditch—with other cars whizzing by, navigating expertly and efficiently. How did they manage to stay focused on the road? They focused on their thoughts on the desired outcome.

Being stuck didn't happen all of a sudden. It was a long process that started with several thoughts, thoughts you had about a certain predicament or life circumstance. These thoughts created the world in which you discover yourself today. How did this happen? With thoughts to which you have devoted an unspecified amount of time, energy and emotion, you began to build a strong belief. As that belief becomes more pronounced you make it a core belief.

Core Beliefs are the foundation on which you base your reaction to life situations. The way you dress, the way you talk, the way you interact with people are all tied to some core belief. **A *core belief*** is something you consider to be absolute and true, and use as a basis, whether verbally or in silent reflection, as a guide to direct every aspect of your life. Just like the foundation of a house—several bricks, then layer upon layer of other materials combine to build the entire structure. Some structures are more solid than others. Have your core beliefs consisted of negative building blocks that will bring your house tumbling down?

Where do core beliefs come from? They come from the people in your life (parents, teachers, associates, siblings), and the environment you live in. They are basically social input. Not all beliefs become core beliefs. Some beliefs come and go like the wind, depending on the situation. Core Beliefs are beliefs that you swear your reputation on, an ideology that you conclude is so true that no one person or thing can change your mind about it.

Core beliefs are like putting gasoline in a luxury car—any kind of gas can make the car run, but putting "premium" in the tank can yield better performance and a smoother ride. What kind of fuel have you been living on? Is it the type of fuel [core belief] that can get you to your destination?

JOURNALING

Articulate in words:

1. Do you consider yourself stuck? If so, how? explain.

____

____

____

2. What thoughts can you change to help you move forward? Explain.

____

____

____

No one keys can fit your car so how can their thoughts fit inside your head?

Chapter 2
What is Stuck?

So let's see what the word ***stuck*** actually means: paralyzed, dumbfounded mystified, perplexed, frustrated, stumped, unable to proceed or move freely, to become jammed or blocked.

Yes, but why am *I* stuck? And what can I do about my problems?

Why? Because you chose thoughts that do not lead to a healthy outcome. Your intentions may be pure but your outcome is muddled.

Most people, when confronted by a challenge or situation in their lives, focus only on the problem. They want to fix the problem, but subconsciously can make it worse. The more they ponder the problem the more energy they give it to grow. Think of a challenge or problem like a seed that is planted deep within the soil, when given water and sunlight. The seed sprouts and continues to grow as long as it is nourished. In the same manner, thoughts allow a problem to grow.

It's the same as fixing a flat tire, then taking the rest of the car apart to make sure the tire *is* the problem. It's no secret that the more you *worry* about a problem the more energy you give to it, the larger it grows. While that's true, if you don't look at the problem and apply some steps at working through it, it won't get solved and may lead to even bigger problems.

What does looking at a problem constantly have to do with *fixing* it? The best way to solve a problem is consider it a *challenge*. Problems have a way of seeming insurmountable. Challenges, with the proper degree of focus can be overcome. Refocus your time, energy and perspective of what it is that you are trying to fix. One way would be to ask yourself, what can I get out of this situation? Why is this lesson here at this moment in time? What am I supposed to learn?

Once you have asked yourself these questions, you will know that *being stuck is only an* ***illusion*** *of not asking the right questions*. For example, if you step back right now and think about how you came to be stuck, you will see that you had a certain pattern of thoughts that lead you to this point. Just like a road map which leads a person to a destination, thoughts have the same effect. Being blinded by past thoughts while trying to fix a situation with time, sweat and tears, meant it did not occur to you to stop and reevaluate the situation. Did you question how the challenge came into existence? Or were you too busy seeing only the problem, not realizing that the answer to your challenge lay just on the other side of the door. .

As you ponder this scenario you may ask yourself, *what is holding me hostage?* Is it past relationships, parents' moral values, teachers' direction, or is it my Karma? (kismet, lot, luck, or fate) How did I get to this place in my life without a blueprint for living life and manifesting my desires and dreams? Now would be the perfect time for you to jot down answers to these questions and examine your core beliefs. Maybe these core beliefs can be exchanged for ones of better value.

So is stuck a state of mind or is it a physical condition?

Both. Physically, you are stuck when you cannot see a way forward. So you sit and waste time, doing nothing but watching television, being in other folks' business, complaining about your friends, job, in-laws, etc. Mentally, you are stuck when you don't ask the right questions to help move you closer to your desire. And you are mentally stuck when you do not seek to change a negative or unsupportive environment.

You must see that there is a different way to achieve that which you are seeking. Whether that is business success or personal desires that you are wanting.

JOURNALING

.

Articulate in words:

1. What, at this point in time, is holding you hostage (captive, victim, prisoner)? Explain.

____

____

____

2. How can you rethink a problem to make it more of a challenge? Explain.

____

____

____

Make a promise to yourself, that you will be responsible for your own happiness.

CHAPTER 3

I'M A GOOD PERSON, WHY AM I NOT SUCCESSFUL?

When people speak about success, you need to have an understanding of what success means to that person. Everyone gauges their success on what is going on in *their* life. No two people will probably agree on what exactly it is. Let's deal with the dictionary definition of **success:** that which meets with, or one who accomplishes, favorable results with family, business, or friends.

Case Study:

Tony is a typical client of mine. He's laid back and easy to talk with. He was not looking for very much coaching but looking for someone he could use as a sounding board. Tony's issues are like that of most people dealing with a 9 to 5 life, job, and boss.

In our sessions what I really wanted to stress to Tony was that, no matter what level of success another person has reached in their career, it should not affect his mission in life. The only way anything someone else said or did could affect him, was if he allowed their energy to become his. In other words, these people he thought were controlling his life could not control what they did not know about. I told him, in this instance, to keep what he was doing to himself, or tell only those whom he really trusted and knew would support him.

Tony walks through his neighborhood on a daily basis, seeing the SUVs, Mercedes and Jaguars being driven by men half his age. These men seemed to be involved in a fast paced lifestyle (commonly called sex, drugs, and rock roll). Tony wonders why he cannot achieve their level of success in his 9-to-5. Tony, never one to live beyond his means, still lives with his mother, drives a car that is held together by pure faith and friction, and has a moderate income. But Tony sits alone and focuses on why he *isn't* as successful as all those other guys he sees.

Suggestion:

First of all, let's discover the object of Tony's focus. Is he focused on other's goal posts? Because if he is, he must now put himself in *their* shoes, since that is the only way he can gauge *his* success is through *their* eyes. Now, if Tony chooses to ponder why he is not successful by looking at *himself*, I would say he is on the right path. Tony must ask himself, where does he truly want to go in life? What does he truly believe about his life? And how does he view moving to the next phase of his life? Second, if Tony can answer these questions truthfully, he is ready to move forth. Now, he must review where he is in his life at the present time, he has to see where he has come from with the intention not to repeat mistakes.

Mistakes? I'm not talking about bad mistakes, I'm talking about *missteps*, so saying the word mistake and hyphenate it as missteps. Where in his life did he take that misstep that led him to this point? If he can review and see that misstep, he should think about what it would have been like to allow himself to be free enough to have taken a different path—a path which would have lead him to a more prosperous end.

That same path can still, with the right focus, lead him to where he believes he should be. But he must remove all the obstacles and stumbling blocks that led to that first misstep. Now I would ask, if Tony can be truthful about that misstep, can he actually go within and give the core reason why? What was the one thing, the one belief that did not allow him to fly? It appears Tony has always had a desire for a more prosperous life. If this desire was not still burning inside, he would not have asked the question why.

Which leads me to the question of being a good person. Many people, just like Tony, also feel that they are owed something strictly because they are a "good person." *Good has nothing to do with what you receive from the Universe.* The Universe sees good and bad or, as I would say, positive and negative, as equals. You have a choice. The Universe only answers and matches the strongest vibration or desire. Even though Tony chose a different path, his original want or desire was still not met. It just was not the predominant desire at the time. Fears and old (core) beliefs and habits overrode the initial desires. But as time went on, Tony's fears began to subside and the desire was able to resurface. To want or desire, you must nurture your dreams. You must hold onto them. As we see here with Tony, he has returned to the initial desire.

One true lesson Tony must understand is that no matter what he sees over his fence he doesn't know the degree of thought, desire, and focus that went into what others have achieved.

Hypothetical case:

You pass by a beautiful woman outside a market place. As she slips into the driver's seat of her brand new silver Mercedes, you observe she's wearing a fur coat, diamonds or other jewels on every finger and Prada shoes. You may stop and say "whoa, how can I live like that?" The person wishing to exchange places with this woman, wouldn't know all the facts behind her seemingly good life. Nor would the person know that, while driving to her mansion, she's thinking about the emotional, physical and verbal abuse of a husband that she will endure for the rest of the day. To her, it appears this man has nothing better to do with his time (outside of making millions) but to mistreat and disrespect her. What price does she pay for the comfort of material things?

Suggestion:

Would you be willing to pay that price to get what you want? Knowing all that you know about this situation, ask yourself, would you want to walk in her Prada shoes? I'm not saying that opulent material items are immoral, but to achieve them on your own is more empowering. Having the pure satisfaction of owning your own is so rewarding. It is the first step in elevating one's self-esteem. Rather than exchanging a part of your soul for the sheer privilege of saying that you own Gucci, (Pucci, or Fearucci); Chanel or Versace, revise your thinking to: "I now do it for myself," "I am strong, and capable of making it *on my own*." I know this sounds a little simplistic, but had this woman been thinking in this vein she would have slowly, but steadily, started to change her mental and physical condition. With that said, she can still achieve exactly what her heart desires. Had she said, "I would like to be rich and powerful, healthy and have peace of mind, what would her outcome have been?"

It all goes back to one person's perception of another person's success. So what I would say is, concentrate and focus on elevating yourself to the next level. Also remember that as good as you say you are, those are only *spoken words*. The goodness has to come from within. You must vibrate that feeling into the Universe and into your space, environment, and your life.

When all is said and done, Tony must surround himself with people that are already achieving the success in life that he desires. Whether that is a career as a stockbroker, banker, lawyer, or even a hockey player—he must interact with those people. Being focused and networking with these role models will help Tony stay on track, for theirs is the lifestyle he seeks. As Tony follows the formula for a change in life, he should write down his experiences and keep a journal about his progress. Keeping a journal allows you to reflect back on the steps you have made. The journal would detail the people he met, where he met them, and his interactions with them. In the journal would also be an account of his feelings about being in an environment in which he had dreamed about. A journal is like a blue print of a building, everyday you can use it to build upon and add the next layer of success.

Listen to your heart, then your head and you will know which way to go.

CHAPTER 4

HOW WILL I KNOW IF WHAT I WANT IS RIGHT FOR ME?

Want is a word that has so many definitions. Let's look at some of them: being in a state of not having; lack; the absence of or the scarcity of what is needed or desired.

What is needed here is a self-analysis test. Ask yourself, "what would I love to do if I could do it right now without negatively affecting my current income?" (Notice I said *current income*. Most people are not willing to leave their *comfort zone* to achieve their desire). What would your answer be? Write a book, open a restaurant, start a bed & breakfast, become a painter, or join the circus? Now that you have a little more insight on what it is that you *want* to do, you need to ask yourself, can I make a living doing this wonderful thing that I have always dreamed of? And if so, how can you bring this dream to fruition? What actions must you take? Would you be willing to go all the way if the place, time, income, and plan of action all comes together? If the final answer is yes, then proceed to color your new career as beautiful as you can using all your senses; touch, hearing, smell, sight, and even taste.

If the answer is *no* to living your dream, then you need to ask yourself, how else might I bring this desire into my life? What would be the key to unlocking the door to your mind and breaking down the barriers that will not let you move forward? Making a list of everything you say no to might be a good place to start. Write down the reasons for saying no. There will probably be more information in the reasons you give, so start there. Ask yourself, where did these roadblocks come from, and do they have a history?

If you don't feel comfortable with the history for your reasons, release them. Start anew with your own beliefs, collecting data on the subject, then critique it for yourself. Form your *own* opinions, then begin.

JOURNALING.

Articulate in words:

1. What do you desire? Explain.

____

____

____

2. Are there any roadblocks? Explain.

____

____

____

3. What would be the key belief to unlocking the door to achieve your goal? Explain.

____

____

____

What is a want? A want is something outside of a need that either can be satisfied through focus or it can fall to the wayside. Because not much energy is expended during a "wanting" it is neither here nor there. It's something that fulfils your flight of fancy. Something that makes you feel good at that time.

Want vs. Desire

Even though these words will be used interchangeably, let's clear the air about the two. Desire is defined as a natural longing, a craving. Want is a state of not having, lack of.

Desire goes beyond want. Even the word itself creates images of deep passion (outside of the kind that stirs your loins). But it is something that can absorb your very soul and bring a great deal of happiness and fulfillment. People sometimes mistake a strong want for a desire. I can say "I want a glass of water," but desire will make me get up, go to the sink, pull down a glass and get it, or do whatever is necessary to get it. The water will remain exactly where it's been since the beginning of time unless you get off your seat and set things in motion.

How will I know if what I desire is right for me?

When people use the word "right," I have to question, what is right? What are you saying? Right for whom and for what? If it is right for you, *you will know*. If not, you will fuss, fight and kick but in the end you will know if it is not right. You will feel awful about doing whatever it is that you are doing, be that a job, relationship, or charity work. It's like trying to wear shoes that are too small for your feet, you will only be able to stand in them for a short period of time before they start to hurt. Those shoes will continue to look good, but you won't be able to fit in them comfortably. The same holds true to whether or not a situation or action is right for you. No need to question—you will know!

Case Study:

I have a Life Coaching client who could fit the bill for almost any man or women I know. Just replace her name for yours and change the sexual description and you will probably see yourself.

Tina's preference in men had always been tall, dark and handsome, with six figure incomes and a generous disposition. She ran into quite a few that fit the bill. Several unhappy years later she met a wonderful man who was short, stocky and bald. His salary was nowhere near six figures, but he had a pleasant personality and exuded a spiritual quality she found attractive. Tina's "desire" made her rule him out. Upon further examination, she found she enjoyed his company, she felt safer with him than with any of the other men she'd been with. Many of Tina's previous relationships turned out to be abusive, controlling or even domineering to a critical degree. Though on some level each man met a condition of what she requested, she just hadn't been specific enough in other areas of her requests.

Suggestion:

After Tina decided to opened up to receive the goodness of the Universe, she finally relaxed and realized that what happened in her life previously was brought on by old thought patterns or core beliefs. Now, it's obvious (at least to us) that the new guy was perfect for her, but in her efforts to hold on to what she *thought* she desired, she almost missed out on her current husband.

Opening up and looking at a situation with unbiased eyes allows for new energy to flow. It is not so much that you have to try everything that comes along, it is allowing yourself to perceive what might be if you take in new information and then act upon it.

JOURNALING

Articulate in words:

1. Think about your current job and life situation. How do you feel? Explain.

____

____

____

2. What old beliefs are you holding onto that are no longer needed?

____

____

____

3. When was the last time you engaged in a new adventure, ate at a wonderful restaurant, enjoyed a stage play or paid a visit to an amusement park? Explain.

____

____

____

Ask the Universe for anything you want, then wait for it in a position of gratitude.

CHAPTER 5
EXPECTANCY

Let's deal with the complete definition of expectancy: the act of expecting or looked for with interest; the object of hope, the possession of which a person is entitled to have, at some future time, which is called anticipation.

Other words that describe expectation are belief, calculation, confidence, anticipation, hope, outlook, presumption, probability, supposition, surmise, and waiting. All these words are straight out of the dictionary. Which word best describes your level of expectancy?

Expectation is a sticking point for some people. Those people don't believe they have a right to a prosperous, beautiful and fulfilling life. It's as if they believe they have to do penance first to see if they are worthy of their desire. There appears to be an "I'm not good enough yet" syndrome, as though their desires and needs in life should be sanctioned by their church, government, parents or peers?. But none of that is true; all that one has to do is to *believe* in their desires and **expect** to have what they want.

In the Bible the phrase **"Ask and you will be given what you ask for"** has been commonly used. It did not say *keep asking*, it said, in paraphrase—ask, prepare, then dig your ditches expecting your rainfall. *So how might one do that?* By holding an image in your mind of what you desire. By holding that image long enough so that your first, second, and on to the eighth thought about your desire all have the same *emotion*, *power* and *energy* to live, and be automatically expected, as being a part of your already existing world.

When you can clearly see yourself having it, the Universe will match those thoughts with an earthly material equivalent. Visualizing that which you desire is good, but it is not great. What is great is when you ***"Act As If"*** (acting as if you already have it). Stop looking at your life as it is now and start looking at how *you want it to be*. Never let go of that vision until it has materialized.

It doesn't matter whether that the end result is a new job, a wonderful significant other, or just peace of mind. It is yours if that is what you desire. But until you can get used to that feeling of having it, you must have a strategy. One strategy would be: cut out pictures and place them in key locations in your house, car, or work place. Any place where you spend a great deal of time. Another would be to write out scenarios of how you are going to enjoy your new desire and where and with whom. Telling trusted friends and family members what you desire is another good strategy to bring about the object of your desire—*if* they share the same positive thought process as you do.

Go about your day as if the car you are now driving *is* the desired one. Whether it is still the old one doesn't make a difference, it is now the new one you wanted. And treating it as such brings about your desires much faster because now it is your *expectation*, and in a thought form the Universe can match. From this point on it looks, smells, and feels like the real deal. Doing this adds to the realization of having the desired object.

Your expectation must be as great as the approach of Thanksgiving, Christmas and New Year's holidays every year.

You know that time of year is coming, and you feel good about it or anxious, or sad but there is a feeling wrapped around it. You will fill in all the spaces of expectancy with the who's, what's and where. What type of feelings, sights, sounds and smells are associated with this expectant time of year? Some might be the trees, the lights, the snow, the holiday parties, the egg nog, and even the smiles on people faces. These types of feelings, visual cues and triggers are called anchors in NLP terminology (Neuro-Linguistic Programming). NLP is the study of reprogramming the mind through language, word, sight, sound and smell if applicable.

These anchors have meaning in your life, they make you remember good things or sad situations, but they do trigger memories. If you are expecting disaster, then that is what you are going to get. The Universe does not differentiate between good or bad expectations, it just matches the *urgency* and the *strength* of the emotion and energy sets forth. Expectation can be a very powerful tool in your toolbox of life. What are you expecting?

JOURNALING

Articulate in words:

1. Are you expecting your desire? If so by doing what? Explain

____

____

____

2. What will it feel like to have your goal or dream? Give a detailed account.

____

____

____

If given a choice take the one that is of the highest good.

CHAPTER 6
DO BLESSINGS HAVE ANYTHING TO DO WITH MOVING FORWARD IN LIFE?

No matter where I go, I'm often asked this question. People seem to feel that if you have more than your share of good, then you've been blessed.

"Everything will work out," most people have said at one time or another. If I have enough *faith* and *trust* in the Universe—all of my desires will come to fruition. Easier said than done. That is only because most people want an outside source to be responsible for their choices in life. Most people will tell you, "I'm Blessed" or that they are *chosen*. Some may call it *well favored*. Well, I'd like to ask: Is not everyone blessed? If so, why doesn't everyone just say *we're blessed*?

Blessing: to express a wish or prayer for the happiness, to confer prosperity or happiness upon. That which promotes prosperity and welfare for all. To praise or glorify; to extol for excellences that which you have received.

When seeing my car, my house, clothes, and the success of my businesses, if a person says, “You’ve been blessed.” I always wondered who’s being left out in the cold. Are blessings to be divvied up and handed out like rewards at a graduation? Are blessings things, situations or states of mind? Some people view it as all three. What they don’t realize is the things that they consider a *blessing*, are in actuality a manifestation of concentrated, focused thought.

A woman who has wanted for her soul mate for years, suddenly finds herself in the presence of the person she knows is just that. Then later, they marry and she blissfully says to anyone who asks, “I’m blessed.” Well, didn’t she recognize that the Universe only delivered that which she asked for? Doesn’t the person who finally purchases the car of their dreams (at a substantially less cost when they originally believed they couldn’t afford it), understand that the Universe was intervening and bringing forth that which they focused upon? But this intervention happens only after the person changed their thought pattern and started to believe the object of their desire was already in their possession. Was that a blessing? Or was it that the person had the foresight to visualize and focus on what they desired?

Maybe what you would call a **blessing** is that which you did not believe the person had the ability to create. When one speaks of blessings, they are actually talking about what they perceived to be theirs and only theirs. If you ever wondered where the word *blessed* comes from, you should look in the dictionary to get a broader prospective of the meaning. But if you are using it generically, then why not set up a system so that people will know what they must do to be blessed? Why not allow everyone to share in the glorious prosperity that is created through blessings? Wouldn’t it be better to just tell everyone that you have received the Divine Order of the Universe? And by that, meaning you know how the laws of the Universe work. So, when you say "I'm blessed," why not say, "and so shall the Universe provide more."

For those who come from a Biblical background these words may sound familiar: Mark 11: 23-24 *For verily I say unto you, that whosoever shall say unto this mountain, be thou removed, and be though cast into the sea, and shall not doubt, and he shall believe that those things which he said shall come to pass. He shall have whatsoever he saith.* Therefore, I say unto you, what things whatsoever ye desire, when ye pray believe that ye receive them and ye shall have them. Psalms 37:3-4 Delight thyself also in the Lord and he shall give thee the desires of thine heart.

Let's talk about *trust*: The first definition should set off bells and whistles: assured resting of the mind on the integrity. The dictionary says ***trust*** is the condition or obligation of one to whom anything is confided. A person or thing to have confidence in. Someone to rely on, to confide, or repose faith, expect with desire. Also, confidence; belief; faith; hope; expectation. Trust moves mountains.

I love when people tell me they "trusted" someone. I follow up with the question, do you trust yourself? Most of the time I get half-hearted answers, like, "I guess I do." Now, if you have so much faith in someone else, why won't you have the same faith in yourself? You are basically asking someone to carry your water and not drop any on the ground, but you have given them a broken vessel. Until you can trust yourself you cannot expect anyone to trust you.

Trust's definition has the word *confidence* in it, and means you are assured of what you are doing or at lest aware of what you are wanting. If you are seeking a trusting relationship in business, family or in friendship, come to the table with some semblance of self-esteem. Without confidence in yourself, you are going to continuously ask the other person to be your anchor in the storm of life. It is impossible for a relationship to survive such a strain on one person, especially if the person is not centered in their own life.

You cannot give what you do not have. So when you ask someone to trust you, **trust** yourself first. Expect that the person you want to trust will deliver only as much as they can, given their situation at the time.

JOURNALING

Articulate in words:

1. Name three ways you feel you are Blessed.

____

____

____

2. Write several ways you have used focused thought to achieve a goal.

____

____

____

Chapter 7
Why does it take so long to get what I want?

Time is of the essence. Time is also the duration of a person's life, the hours and days to which a person has at their disposal. But when you are dealing with a person's belief system you must know where their starting point is. Are they on target? Are they mentally comprehending their power to achieving their goals? Have they set their sights too high or too low? These are the questions that should be answered.

How long will it take before you see your desire? There is no set time for your desire to appear.

Suggestion:

You must ***act as if*** you already have it. How you say? **By cleaning out your closets** making room to receive the desire. When I speak about cleaning out your closets, I'm not talking about a broom and a mop type of cleaning (although . . .). What I'm talking about is the way your life is filled with clutter and the way you have closed your life to other ways of attacking a problem. Cleaning out your closets can be so refreshing and exhilarating, and a way to review the current situation in your life.

Take account of what you have stored away in the recesses of your mind. This will help you to rid yourself once and for all, of things which have nothing to do with where you want to go. Start cleaning out your closet by *removing people and things that no longer fit the life that you desire*. Stop going to places with "friends" that you really could care less about. Stop doing chores that you deem unnecessary.

When you finish cleaning out your closets, you will instantly be aware that the phone has stopped ringing. The "maid service" you provided to friends and family will all but dissipate. People will no longer dump their dirty laundry, baggage, negative energy on your doorstep. You will feel a purging of old stress and anxiety as it rushes from your body. You may feel an overwhelming need to cry or just sit and ponder why you put yourself through these debilitating obligations in the first place.

Making the decision to move forward is not easy. It is hard to let go of being an **enabler**. An enabler is one who allows another person to lean on them for all of their needs. Now is the time to allow yourself to set in motion the key to unlock the door to your freedom. So when I say clean out your closet, I'm talking about setting up boundaries for everyone with whom you interact. Do not put anything in your closet that you cannot use to move closer to your goals. When you are moving about your everyday life, do not look at things and say that person/object has potential. If you cannot truly use it while you are on your march toward your dream, goals and desires leave it exactly where you found it.

So when you clean out your closets, get rid of all that is conducive to your moving vehemently forward. It may take a little time, but if you make a worksheet, you can go down the list and slowly eliminate all those items that will not work for you any longer.

How might you start? First follow the steps mentioned above, then ***"Act As If"*** you already have your desire so you will be able to manage it when you do acquire it. Over and over you will hear me repeat this step because it is so important that you understand the power of your mind to bring you anything you can imagine.

Have you ever known a lottery winner? Statistics show that most of the winners are broke within 2 to 3 years of receiving their winnings. Why? Because they never made room for all the *new* coming into their lives. If the mind isn't prepared for the new, it will resort to old ways of thinking, old ways (or core beliefs) that can not supply the new (money).

Contrary to popular belief you must be expecting what is about to happen in your life or you will just lose it. I know you say, "well I know someone who won the lottery, and they weren't even *thinking* about it." That is what's called a quantum leap.

Let me clarify that by saying your friend may have been thinking about a car, a house or taking a vacation to an exotic island. Just by *thinking* and *dreaming* about those things and seeing and smelling the newness of it all can bring their desire into existence. The lottery was just a vehicle for fulfilling that desire. A gut feeling or intuition may have convinced her to stop at the store or gas station to buy a soda and upon seeing the lottery advertisements decided, why not? And therein lies the quantum leap. But it wasn't about her winning the lotto, it was about her *desire* to do several things, such as owning a home, taking a vacation or buying a new car.

Consider what time frame you're dealing with. What are your time constraints? What are your deadlines? Now, if one plants a seed, do you expect to see the flower the very next day? The next week? Have you given your desire as much attention as you would give a plant? Have you nurtured it? Have you watered it? Have you brought it into the sunlight? While I'm speaking in metaphors, I just want to clarify that you need to spend a lot of time nurturing that wilted flower, just as you would a wayward desire.

Now let's expand my thoughts on this subject. Much time is needed to nurture the whole garden. The amount of care that is given to that single wilted plant will pay off in the end. A desire needs your attention daily, if not hourly, to yield visible results. Are you even ready to receive your desire? If so, this life-changing component that is called your desire will come to you without warning.

Case study:

This is not a client of mine, but the son of a client. She was another worried mother wanting some insight about what was going on with her teenage son. This is one of those stories that most adults don't remember. They have forgotten they had growing pains when they lived at home with their parents.

Brandon was once an honor roll student who, in his first year of high school, performed significantly lower than expected. No amount of pushing, prodding, or fussing changed the outcome and even he believed that he wouldn't graduate from school.

When Brandon went on a college tour with his class and became *exposed* to the wonderful aspects of college life, he decided he wanted to go college out of state. Suddenly there was a transformation in the way he viewed school, his teachers and the learning experience. There were no more days of arriving late to school; he didn't need any encouraging to seek the help he needed. Now, Brandon has a 3.5 average and has received a four-year academic scholarship to the college of his choice.

Suggestion:

Being ready has a great deal to do with receiving the desire. It is the same as a hand being closed tightly: nothing can penetrate or get in. But once the mind expands, and the hand opens, *one can receive just about anything they desire.* **They** have to make sure they stay focused on their dreams, desires and goals or whatever is placed in their hands.

Too much clutter in a person's life can keep desires at bay. If what you desired came when you actually wanted it—where would you put it? Some people's lives are so filled with clutter—in the relationships, family life, home and just plain old baggage—that they have no place to put anything else. They can desire all they want, but if there is no room, it will remain in the Universe until there's space free and it can find a permanent home with one who is ready for it.

For Brandon, it didn't take all that long for him to turn his life around. Initially, his bottom line was: I'll do this because it's expected. Then he changed, because it wasn't his desire but everyone else's. The moment he said he wanted to control his life, he changed the patterns of his thoughts. Outside of his parent's and teacher's control, his desire for success was sparked. This is called **contrast** at its best. From what you don't want, you look to see what you *do* want.

Knowing what you don't want only works if you don't stay on that page. Focus only from that point on what you *do* want, then turn the page.

Brandon looked at his situation and decided that in order to make a change, he would have to reevaluate the way he perceived attending school. It is almost as if he said, what could I use this school for other than a place to hang out? His answer: This will be my place to hatch new ideas. I will learn about life. Whether I succeed at my true goal of controlling my own life at this time, I will use these tools presented to me in this school, to project and develop my will. And just like Brandon—you can expand your mind and open up to the Universe, then allow your destiny to unfold.

JOURNALING

Articulate in words:

1. What clutter are you holding onto in your life? How can you get rid of it or let it go? (This can be a situation, inanimate object or people) Explain.

____

____

____

2. Are you ready at this moment to receive your desire or goal? Explain

____

____

____

CHAPTER 8
CAN I WANT FOR SOMEONE ELSE?

In the Metaphysical world the word "Want" can be very debatable. (Meta means above and beyond, and physical means material or that which is experienced by your five sense). Is wanting more powerful than desire? In corporate America, the word, "want" is used to mean not necessary to the bottom line of business because it is not a need. So when I use the word want in this context it is neither less or more than desire.

Spending time working on other people's issues can slow down your journey and cause you to lose sight of your goals and desires.

Yes, you can want for someone else, but the question is whether what you are wanting for someone else is what he or she needs in their lives. No one knows for sure what another person needs in their life unless and until they actually sit down and have a heart to heart talk with them. Your wanting for the person will not make a change. Your degree of want has to be matched by *their* degree of desire. You cannot want to a degree that will change that person's environment or alter their path. This all stems from the individual.

On the lighter side, you may say, I want that for that person. That's basically you being Benevolent, wanting that person to be happy. But when it comes to a point of wanting more than the person actually desires, the two will never synchronize.

JOURNALING

Articulate in words:

1. What do you want for someone that they do not want for themselves? Explain?

____

____

____

2. How do you think this person would react knowing that you wanted a desire for them? Explain?

____

____

____

Praying

Prayer is of different kinds one is the act of communicating with a deity. Dictionaries also define ***prayer*** as an earnest or urgent request. Prayer also can be broken down to include but not exclude the following definitions; invocation, plea, proposal, proposition, address, a questions or a submission and my personal best ASKING. You may have heard stories of people saying that they prayed someone back to health. Praying and wanting are so different that the two cannot be put in the same category. Praying is more of a spiritually focused energy, one that is looked upon as a healing device. When you're praying for someone, usually the person is already in a state of desiring wellness and happiness. By the other person focusing on being whole is what puts them in sync with your prayers. So when you ask the person who wants to be whole again, what is your prayer? This unites your prayer with the recipient desire and its allows you to pray their request.

When two or more gather together in my name I will be in the mist of thee. Matthew 18:20

JOURNALING

1. What prayer do you say for others? Explain.

____

____

____

2. What prayer do you pray daily? Write it out

____

____

____

Worrying:

Worrying is the flip side of praying. Worry is a constant nagging in the pit of your stomach to do something about nothing. The dictionary explains **worry** as anything causing distress or worry or anxiety, thinking moodily or anxiously about something. My definition is that worry disturbs your peace of mind. How clear can the words be about what worrying does to your physical and spiritual body? *If you are centered and at peace with yourself you cannot have room for worry.* If you had your plan mapped out in your journal, why would anxiety creep in? It appears that the only time you would be that filled with anxiety is when you have just achieved one of your desires and didn't know which one to start on next. **That is the point to start all over, using new blueprints and worrying still wouldn't factor into it.**

Remember, when you worry you cannot have peace of mind. And when there is no peace of mind, you are not connected to your "Source." Without peace of mind, you will feel unrest and be out there in a "raw and ragged" state. Even the Bible has this to say on the subject: A double-minded man is as unstable in all his ways." James 1:8, You will feel as if no one cares about you and that you are on your own without any help or guidance. If you are not connected to "Source energy," you are not able to feel or hear the wonderful sounds of the Universe.

JOURNALING

Articulate in words:

1. What do you worry about and why?

___

___

___

2. Does worrying feel good? If not, is there another way you can use your time *instead* of worrying? Explain.

___

___

___

3. Do you have a life plan? If so, in what ways have you demonstrated your desired outcome? Give a full description.

___

___

___

To become one with yourself will leave you free of someone else's voice.

CHAPTER 9
WHY CAN'T I STAY FOCUSED WHEN OBSTACLES ARISE?

So you ask, what is **focus**? A point of concentration, **focus** is a degree of clarity—clarity that one has when they are looking to perform a certain task or attain a certain goal. So, when you ask, what is focus? It is being able to concentrate so intently that you can achieve your goal to the point that nothing interrupts you.

Focus has varying degrees; it's like being able to multi-task. There will always be something that will hold the majority of your attention. This concentrated attention becomes your *focus*. Attention is the base for focus and out of that attention, the focus grows and becomes clear. If you look around your environment, there are a lot of interesting things that can hold your attention for a certain period of time. But it's when you give your *full, unadulterated attention to something* that it now becomes a focus.

It's like looking through glasses that have smudges. They are blurry and hard to see through. But when the desire comes for you to get a really clear look, you will take them off and wipe them clean, because now there's something important to *see*. That is what focusing is about, being able to chose what it is you want to see. If you want to tune into something bad enough, you'll do it. There are no ifs, ands, or buts about it, you will find away to stay on point.

As I mentioned in a previous chapter, one way you might do this is to take pictures of your desire and post them about your house. Post the pictures in places that you frequent the most, like the bathroom, the kitchen or in your car. This technique can be used whether it is a relationship you desire, a job for which you have been interviewing for, or a vacation you have been putting off because you just "can't find the time or the money." Focus some degree of attention on the object of your desire everyday.

Another great technique one can use is to ***"Act as if."*** I talked about this before, but it is important to note that *acting as if you already have what you want* shows you are mentally prepared to receive it. This is such a good way to achieve your goals because it allows you to see your desired outcome before it manifests itself. Now allow these pictures to become your anchor, your port in a storm, small but yet resilient enough to shelter the onslaught of winds, rains, and sun.

Okay, you want me to explain more on ***Acting as if.*** The common question is: What if someone sees me *acting as if* I have a new car and I don't? Does it really make a difference what another person thinks? You are here to have a fulfilling life and serve your higher purpose, not to become one with those who really don't care what you are doing the moment you step away from them. They couldn't tell you what you were wearing the day before, much less tell you what you were doing and saying while you were acting as if.

Acting as if, is so important to the process of receiving all that you desire. It all has to do with reprogramming yourself: mind, heart, body and soul. ***Acting as if*** separates what you want from frivolous dreams and things that you do not want. If you ***act as if***, you are committing to being seen as someone who doesn't have all their screws fastened tightly. Your intentions now are committed to the process of manifesting the material presence of your desire.

Now let's connect to that desire. Do you *really* want it, or do you just say things like: "that would be nice to have, "or "that would look great in my house, but I really can't see myself in possession of something like that?" Or, "I don't have the money right now to purchase it." ***Acting as if*** calls for no money, it just calls for total commitment from yourself. Is that work? Yes! But it is also work to go out and get a second job or to work overtime to afford the desire? Whether it is a vacation or a new house, all you have to do is *see* it, *desire* and *be* it. Take your pick: physical labor or mental focus . . .

Setbacks are refueling stations

Chapter 10
What are obstacles?

Obstacles are anything that stand in your way and must be circumvented or surmounted. The lack of imagination is a major obstacle to one's advancement. Obstacles, in this sense, would be the things that keep you from focusing: family, friends, jobs, relationships, and children.

Case Study:

I'll call her "Natasha;" she represents so many of my clients and friends. Her story is typical, Natasha, a 30 year old fashion consultant, has a motto that says "living for the moment." She has immersed herself with her friends, excessive partying and "living the good life." This attitude has kept her from moving toward her goals, dreams and aspirations of owning her own business. Then after she has wined, dined, partied and dwindled away pressure time, she asks the question, *why I am stuck?*

Suggestion:

The obvious answer would be: your focus is not on the things you want. Your focus is on temporary pleasures that only fill the void for a short time. One might ask, well, what's wrong with living for the moment?" There's nothing wrong with that if you have a life plan or goal that is achievable and absorbs the better part of your time. But let's be real: living for the moment *does* absorb a great deal of a person's time. There is no focus on anything but pleasure.

There's nothing wrong with partying either, but at the end of the day, you must see your outcome. It's like trying to get driving directions from the Internet without stating a destination. You will not know how long it will take to get there, the road to take, if will there be any detours, sudden construction, or even if the place you are heading still exists.

Case Study:

Here's another one of my clients I'll call her Chelsea, any one of my other clients that are singer/entertainers would fit so well in this scenario. Something unfortunate happens when mixing business with a personal relationship. Chelsea, a jazz singer, aspires to regain status as a "bankable" artist, opening act or headliner. She continues to trudge through life, barely able to make a living. After several years of being stuck, she asks, why haven't I made the "big-time?"

Her intimate relationships absorb a great deal of her energy, creativity and time, limiting her ability to align herself with the right people in the entertainment industry. She loses focus as her "mate" demands more and more of her time, and she watches as her career wanes and dissipates.

Suggestion:

On a day-to-day basis the average person will encounter obstacles in every aspect of their lives and some will be the people you expect to be in your corner.

Scenario 1: The woman who wants to start her own business, will find opposition from family members who had previously supported her.

Scenario 2: The tenant, who finds a jewel of a deal on an apartment in a more upscale neighborhood, suddenly finds the sweet, little old lady landlord decided to put a negative mark on her credit report to keep from losing a good-paying tenant.

Scenario 3: The secretary who decides to go back to school to further her education, soon finds more work piled onto an already large plate.

Topping off all these seemly difficult situations is:

Scenario 4: The person, who normally keeps accurate accounts of their money, and saves every spare penny, now they suddenly have car repairs, tax issues, and medical bills that appear, changing their outlook, while taking the focus off their immediate goals.

The question stills remains—why can't I stay focused when obstacles arise? One reason is most people are not sure if they really want what they say they want. So it's easy not to be focused. It's easy not to see clearly. It's easy to become sidetracked—an escape mechanism to avoid dealing with the pressure of completing the project you're working on. Any little distraction is welcomed by the mind.

The reason you can't stay focused? When you look at what you desire, the outcome seems impossible for various reasons. In all likelihood, one reason is that when you were young you observed the way the adults around you achieved (or failed to achieve) their goals. Whatever you were taught then about goals, plays a big part now. *Even though you don't consciously think about it, in the back of your mind you're still programmed to believe that you cannot have it—or don't deserve it.* Now is the time to start replacing those thoughts or core beliefs with new ones. Thoughts of fulfillment that reflect how you would feel once you had that which you desire. Reprogram yourself; allow yourself to try a new way of viewing your life desires. Reading books on setting goals, listening to tapes and CD's or attending seminars give you more insight on changing your approach. Doing this on all levels can be useful and is a better way to experience the desire, seeing it, smelling it, feeling it, and tasting it, if possible.

Case study:

I know a lot business people will identify with Leslie's story

Leslie, a 40-year-old Executive Account Director at a major advertising agency consistently remains "stuck" and unfocused because her mind has detoured into several different areas. She has several projects in the works, which dilute her focus and energies. She has helped many colleagues and co-workers achieve their dreams and attain a higher level of prosperity. Yet she remains caught in a loop doing the same thing over and over again. Just like a hamster runs around the treadmill every day, all day—the same thing, the same scenery, the same results.

Suggestion:

Maybe this is because she is not sure how any one of the projects will turn out. When she questions: why am I not famous? why haven't I received the recognition I deserve? she is left wondering about previous decisions, and is unable to voice a valid reason. Once Leslie delved into what she thought were obstacles and rearranged her focus, energy and time in just one project, she realized it was her turn to experience exactly what she desired. In time, in her mind she became clearer and the obstacles dissipated. Her motto became "it's my turn."

One reason people allow obstacles to keep them from their goals, is that they can't see their own greatness. Instead, they resort to looking back through past windows in their life trying to see their greatness or moments of greatness. They need only to realize their purpose in life and be content in who they are *right now* and stay on their path. *It's "cute" to help people, but when you don't have your own, how can you find time to support someone else's dreams and desires.* An example would be: two people who are in a boat and neither one knows how to swim. One falls into the water, does it make sense for the one left in the boat to jump right in? The best thing to do is to throw them a life preserver and row to shore and get help.

The more you become aware of who you are, the greater your signal into the Universe. The greater the signal, the greater the connection.

JOURNALING

Articulate in words:

1. What obstacles stand in your way at this moment in time? Explain.

____

____

____

2. Are you unknowingly creating these obstacles to keep you from your goals? Explain.

____

____

____

3. Describe, in as much detail as possible, what a life free of obstacles would entail. Explain.

____

____

____

People will spend more time on their grocery list than they do on their goals.

CHAPTER 11

WHAT ARE YOU WILLING TO GIVE UP, IN ORDER TO SUCCEED?

Another word that needs clarification is **succeed.**

Which means to achieve, to earn, and to make it to the top. To become rich, famous, to gain, accomplish and to also flourish. Since everyone can identify with or understand success, let's start with one of the reasons people don't succeed.

FEAR

Out of all the reasons for being "**stuck**," fear may be the number one reason. The dictionary definition for **fear** is frightening in itself: an emotion experienced in anticipation of some specific *pain* or *danger,* usually accompanied by a desire to flee or fight. Whether real or imagined, fear leaves you with an anxious feeling. Not forgetting the painful emotion or passion brought about by the expectation of damnation by fear. Then there is the apprehension of impending danger to oneself.

Fear is another four-letter word, almost as powerful as any other four-letter obscenity. Fear is unquestionably one of the main reason people do not succeed in the corporate world or any other world where it's calls for a person to think on their feet. It is one of the hardest things for people to release.

By living with fear, you cut yourself off from living a complete, invigorating life. There is no way you can be connected to the Universe when you are in a state of fear.

What actually happens when someone is in a state of fear is that they cannot see the outcome of the situation they are faced with. Sometimes there isn't even a situation yet, but only a perceived "what if." I cannot count how many talented people I have run across in my life who are stuck because they are fearful. Afraid of what people say, afraid of life, afraid of not being able to control their life. Fear has caused a great many people to become sick and psychotic because they can't see a way to control, that which is presented before them. This is basically how man has dealt with a lot of his problems: if I cannot fix it or know what is in store ahead, then I shall fear it. This has a lot to do with how man wants to be seen, in a light of knowing his surrounding and being in total control. People have a perception of themselves and feel this ought to be met, before they can deal with that which seems unfamiliar or foreign.

Fear causes so many desires not to be met and causes so much chaos in the heart of man. When a desire is not met it shows itself in another form, that of unnourished energy. From this weakened energy comes cancer and possibly other ailments. When I use the word cancer. I use it not as a medical term, but more in the connection of spreading an uneasiness in the soul. Fear has to be the biggest stumbling block for the human condition.

Fear can cause people to falsely accuse another of crimes they did not commit. Fear can cause fighting among the best of friends, family or significant others without rhyme or rhythm. All one needs to know is they felt threatened, which is a form of fear. Fear has so much control in a person's life that it would do a person good to never have to say the word fear. Nothing that has to do with the word should be spoken, or brought into your thoughts, because as it is spoken, so shall it appear.

A better way to talk about the feeling you have when you are not sure about something, which is unknown, is to call it the **"Universe's bigger plan."** "I don't know what it is, but I know it can't hurt me." That sounds great ,you say, but what if I'm a young woman, walking down a dark street and I see men that don't look like **they** are going to be friendly. You must always know that you are divinely protected. That being the case, would you put yourself in a situation where you would not feel good or safe? Remember, every thought has a plot. And if you have already written fear or a situation that brings fear, into the script—then that is exactly how things might play out.

Have you ever watched a movie and knew the ending? You knew the plot; you knew every step the actors were going to make. Then in the same fashion, write your own life script. Know where and how you want your life to go. Even with that, I would say let the Universal Energy help guide you to a better situation. Do not fall into the trap of fear, because then you lose your sense of self. If you do not have sense of self, you will be swept up into a negative energy vortex and you'll forget everything you know about self-protection and survival.

There is another saying: FEAR is false energy appearing real. Tell yourself that whenever you feel fearful. Whether or not it helps you, at least it gives you something to remember and hang your hat on. If you remember that fear has no place in your life, you will know that where there's fear there is no faith. Having faith in your ability to see a glorious outcome. Having enough faith in your ability to know that nothing can bring you harm. Unless you have been sending out unclear vibrations about fear, there is nothing to fear. Just like animals on a certain level can sense fear in humans, your fearful vibrations can be sensed and will bring some type of reaction, possibly not the one you want.

You are truly the captain of your own destiny and only you

can guide your ship into a safe, secure port. The next time you are dealt a hand of fear, what are you going to do? Sit and wait for the dealer to give you more cards or get up and go to another game, one that you know better? Or are you going to stay and "sweat it out" as the dealer turns over one card after another laying your life in front of you and at each moment you feel you have no control.

So you say, "now you are talking about control." Hasn't this whole section on fear really been about controlling the unknown? Has this conversation been about being in control of how you see life, control of how you accept life and how you form your perceptions from what you are viewing? Fear is what fear is, that which is unknown to us at the time a decision is to be made. Whether a business decision, or a decision to run from a scary situation, it's still a desire to control the unknown. If you allow fear to control you, you will soon see that it will take over everything in your life. Fear will make you think that people are talking about you or that people are looking to bring you to your doom.

Fear has no real place in your life, it was once used for the purposes of making one aware of their surroundings but that was when people dwelled in caves. Cave men needed to know what animals to avoid. They needed a mechanism inside of their head that would signal to them: *this is not a good situation—run!* You do not need the same signals anymore. You have developed your reasoning skills and elevated your senses to perceive hidden danger and there aren't that many wild animals running around anymore. (Although, some who are still on the dating scene, might say otherwise.)

The next time you find yourself in a fearful situation, one that you cannot control, and your adrenaline is pumping, *stop* for a few minutes. See if you can't come up with a winning outcome that would suit you. See the situation the way you want it. Then state it **as if** you have already achieved the desired outcome to your advantage. There is nothing more liberating than knowing that you have control over your destination.

Case Study:

In this scenario a client deals with a little more complex situation of fear and self-doubt, but we worked through it. Amy was my metaphysical client, a study which is near and dear to my heart. It was easy for me to understand where Amy was coming from, because I too had been in the same situation.

Amy started a job with a company and things were very rocky in the beginning, almost prompting her to leave within the first month, eventually, things mellowed out and her environment became peaceful. A year later, Amy was offered a job with another company, one with more benefits and better pay. Anyone would jump at the chance. But Amy hesitated, unsure if she should accept the new offer, since things were now so pleasant at her current job. She immediately went into a state of confusion, not knowing which way to go.

In her confusion, Amy forgot one very important thing: at her present job, she learned something about releasing and letting go. Amy created an ideally peaceful environment through meditation and visualization. These same empowering tools would also serve her well in her *new* environment, if she chose to use them. But Amy fell into the trap of fear and self-doubt. Doubt and fear which she knew so well, before she started meditating and visualizing, was revisited. Her seeming comfort with the feeling of fear was exceedingly surprising. Amy would address her fears as friends, calling them by name, and joking about which one would come to visit with her.

Suggestion:

The path of awareness is less traveled. Learning to relax, and recognizing the lessons allows us to release the fear. Amy didn't have to stick around and be a part of the "peace" process at her old place anymore. She could say, "it looked good, felt good, I did it, and now I can move on."

She now had more empowering tools in her toolbox with which to operate and create a better environment, in her new space or wherever she chose to go. Amy has now moved on to her new position and life. She is excited about the exploration.

In order to succeed you must understand that if there seems to be something holding you back. You must face it, then decide to move on. Constantly feeding the beast of fear and self-doubt does nothing to set you on your path of life. When people read the title of this chapter "What are you willing to give up in order to succeed" some believed I was talking about giving up cocktails, smoking and drinking. Even though ridding the body of those substances may help your health, that was not what I meant. I referred to the past or the "ball and chain" that has wrapped itself around your legs.

In order to achieve success, you must look at your life and ask yourself, is this the life I really want? and What am I doing about it? *Why can't I see what I'm doing to myself and those that are around me?* Another question you must ask yourself, *When is the right time to change?* Should you wait for the new job or should you constantly work on your on path in life to the betterment of yourself and others. Success is just another name for all that is given to those who have the faith to strike out a new path for others and yourself. Again I would ask, where is the substance in all that you do to succeed? Where is the *you* in what you do? Are you going to be a puppet for those who have degrees but chose to lock out those who have a better message? When do you say yes to your dreams? Or do you want only for the want of it all? How is your *inner spirit*? Is it intact? Would you be happy to introduce it to the world? Maybe you should just ask yourself, am I the one that truly wants to succeed or am I in this for an ulterior motive?

So to succeed is just as important as knowing who you are. Now put yourself in another person's position. One who has succeeded and now controls the very environment that you are in. Maybe they want you to succumb to them. Would you chose to do it? If you were "in a mode to succeed" you could control the situation and bring about a change without words. This is done through total mind control. What I mean by *total mind control*, is a process of only focusing on the solution you want to achieve. Look at the person as if they only exist as you see them in your mind. Never fall prey to their thoughts or action. I want you to go about your day as you normally would. Be happy, carefree and joyful as you do this. A continual exercise in this form of thought will lead you where you want to go, and transform your way of thinking. It will also change your environment. Just like redecorating an old house, you know exactly how you want it step by step. Now you start to scrape off the old layer of paint and even add new wallpaper; next you lay the new wood floors, tile or linoleum. This is a lot of physical work in an effort to achieve the result of remodeling your home, without a plan. Instead of using a contractor, do this simple exercise in your mind. Let's call this mind redecorating which is the same as total mind control. The names of these two exercises are not a important as you staying focused on your desired outcome. Use mind redecorating anytime and anywhere you feel the space you are in is not conducive to the kind of life you desire.

JOURNALING

Articulate in words:

1. What are you willing to give up to succeed? Explain.

____

____

2. Whose desires and goals are you attempting to fulfill? Are they yours?

____

____

3. Use *mind redecorating* to look at your current situation. Now make it the way you would like to see it. Write down the outcome.

____

____

why do you need a second opinion when the first one is yours?

CHAPTER 12
YOU DON'T NEED THEIR APPROVAL. WHO ARE THEY ANYWAY?

What is approval? Acceptance as satisfactory. The act of giving validity. We seek approval to satisfy our desire to be loved.

If someone approves of some event or occurrence that happens in our lives, we feel *appreciated*. Whether this appreciation comes from our parents, spouse or friends, we feel acceptance: "I did something and they're pleased."

Why we look outside ourselves for this approval is one of the mysteries of life that plays out everyday in our world. It is like being in grade school and the teacher passes out stars. Stars were, even then, classified in order of acceptance—gold, silver, bronze, etc. So all the students are anxiously waiting to see who will get the "gold star."

Most people don't believe that they need anyone's approval. But have you ever asked someone at one time or another: "how do I look?" Yes? There you have it! For those who are self-assured, the phrase would have been "I look good, don't I!" with a big smile. When you are sure of yourself and sure of your path in life you don't look for or seek another's approval.

Acknowledgment is different from approval. Allowing someone else to say you look great does not change who you are, nor the mood, or spirit you are in at the time. Seeking approval can paralyze your life, because you become dependant upon others to tell you whether you are doing the right thing at the right time. And just like sitting in the driver's seat of a car waiting for someone to give you the keys so you can rev it up and hit the road; surely you can't believe you can live your life waiting on someone else to give you the keys to life.

Ask yourself, Do I know what I know now because someone gave me the knowledge, or did I go out and seek it for myself? Is there any time that approval from another is necessary? Yes, from your employer if you work for someone who wants a task performed in a certain manner. But other than that why would you seek another's approval when they are on the path of life the same as you?

"To whom much is given, much is required." But you cannot give if you are waiting for someone to approve of what you are giving. Who loses out? Is it the poor man on the street or the old woman that could have used that old coat of yours to stay warm? Tell me, if you wait (when it is something as simple as physically cleaning out your closets to make room for new things), what will happen to the churches and the shelters of the country? Waiting for someone to approve of your next steps may come too late. If you still want approval, then ***approve of yourself*** and how you want to live your life.

Now say to yourself: "there is no one above me other than the Universe." If this is the case, *how can anyone give you the approval you crave other than the Universe?* I often use the term "who are they" anyway? It is just my way of really finding out who are these Universally-appointed, highly evolved, all knowing intelligent people that are keeping a person from moving forward.

When one digs a little deeper you may find that the "persons" most are talking about are their own fears. And what they were looking for was a way to put off the choice of making a decision that took the energy of a self- assured, self-aware, and confident person. How might you look at approval? Well, when you seek approval it shows that you are not sure about yourself, *so how can anyone be sure about you!*

Here's an example of someone trying to gain approval and expectancy:

Case Study:

For years, "Melanie" struggled with gaining acceptance from her domineering mother. Melanie, a nationally best-selling author, had the admiration and love of her adoring readers and most critics. But the one person whose approval she wanted the most eluded her. Eventually, Melanie's need for her mother's approval changed. She then released the need and the stress of wanting it. She stopped altering her life to gain the approval. As soon as Melanie didn't seek her mother's approval, when it no longer mattered to Melanie anymore, she received it. When in actuality, Melanie's mother was giving her the approval she sought all along. The approval was not shown in the form Melanie thought it should. Melanie, in her quest for approval, didn't recognize it, understand it and completely overlooked it,.

Sometimes we are so concerned about the way approval is supposed to look, and the package it should come in, that part of ourselves which craves approval totally misses the picture.

Suggestion:

People have a tendency to label exactly how approval should be given—what color is it? What size is it? What shape is it? How will it sound? Who writes the standards on how to get approval, anyway? Some people turn their lives over to other people to dictate what, how and when they should feel. That is like letting someone else write the screenplay to your life, while you sit and anticipate the outcome. Then as you read the screenplay you want to cry, because they have given you a script that you can't live up too. Wouldn't it just be easier to accept the fact that you don't need anyone's approval other than your own and your Creator's.

Where is it written, get approval from friend, family, and spouse and then move forth?

Most people have not taken the time to become whole within themselves and are constantly looking to sources outside of themselves for acceptance and an understanding of who they are and what they believe.

In the case of spouses, it is commonly said that two people make a whole. In all reality, how can a person who *isn't* whole themselves, condone or approve of another person? People are not fractions, they are spiritual beings equipped with the tools and mechanisms to evolve into highly intelligent, self-sufficient, well-rounded seekers of truth. Two halves do not make a whole when there are two humans involved. For example a man searching for his soul mate, in his mind is 50% complete. The person he gravitates to is about 75%, complete. The man is searching for the other 50%, while the woman is searching for the other 25%. This means both are searching outside themselves for other people or material things to make themselves "complete." Instead, they should go within to do what it takes to become whole before entering into a relationship.

The fact that they come into the relationship with a mentally or spiritually "incomplete" status will be the basis of many problems, as one will blame the other for their unhappiness or for not "completing" them. By not being whole, you create an opening, a vacuum, and the Universe does not allow for empty spaces.

Think of yourself as a cup, when the water in the cup is not filled to the top, there is room for something else. Whether those empty spaces are filled with love, light, or negativity, it does matter to the Universe, as long as it is being filled. What does matter is that *you* chose to fill your cup. Because if you are not filling it with much needed love, understanding and Infinite Wisdom, anyone can come fill your cup with who and what *they* are--whether you need it or not and whether you like it or not.

Take, for instance, a married woman whose cup is not full, and she has a strong-willed girlfriend who abhors her spouse. Chances are conflicts for her attention will arise and her marriage will be tested.

Or the domineering husband, who marries into a family, but abhors the mother-in-law because she wants to continue to control her submissive daughter. Now there is a major dilemma. In the first case, if the married woman allows the negativity of her friend to fill her cup, the woman may turn against her spouse. And in the second case, if the spouse fills the cup, the wife may turn against her mother.

In your quest to become whole, does not filling your cup with self-love sound better than allowing someone to pour mud into it? Whoever fills the cup gains control of the mind, and hence, your life. Whose cup is it anyway? Filling your cup on your own, with your own truths and desires can bring a sense of peace and you no longer needs to search for answers outside of thosealready springing forth from your inner self.

There are many ways to find who you are through work, art, literature, music, and the earth. We look for it in other people (Who, quiet as it's kept, also happen to be looking, too!), when it should be a spiritual journey. The spirit, the ever-flowing part of the Universe that connects all of us and every living thing and inanimate object, must fill us.

The same scenario is seen in families where the parents, in some ways look to their children for approval. Children are seen as an extension of themselves and the upward mobility of the next generation. When a child succeeds the parent feels an elated sense of self or accomplishment. When the child fails, the parent takes it as a personal affront to their methods of rearing. The cycle of seeking approval continues, from birth to death and back again. Now the children of this unit have learned how to seek approval for everything they do in life.

So when you ponder the occurence of what happens when two people get together who both are in a position of need or seeking approval" Is it not obvious? This type of relationship can only lead to a devastating ending for all involved, including children, parents, and friends.

JOURNALING

Articulate in Words:

1. From whom do you seek approval, and why?

___

___

___

2. Is their approval necessary for you to achieve your goals in life? Explain.

___

___

___

3. If you didn't have their approval could you still be successful?

___

___

___

4. Is there another way you could satisfy your need for approval? Explain.

___

___

___

CHAPTER 13

WHY DO THESE THINGS/ PEOPLE THAT CAUSE ME PAIN KEEP COMING INTO MY LIFE?

It is because you are constantly seeking outside approval and you are not looking inside of yourself for the love. You want someone or something to give you admiration, affection and love.

This is a simple question but there is a complexity of answers.

Before I go any further into the case study, let's define ***pain;*** something or someone that causes trouble. It is also a source of unhappiness. The pain of loneliness is a feeling that people try to avoid. It is also a somatic sensation of acute discomfort. You now have a better understanding of the word ***pain*** in the context that I will discuss in the case study.

Case Study:

Miriam is another one my Life Coaching clients. She is someone who was seeking attention and love. She struggled for years to deal with what happened between she and her uncle. What she wanted was love and attention. She started sending out silent signals for someone to love her and give her some attention, any kind of attention. It turned out to be the wrong attention.

Miriam, a beautiful 36-year-old legal secretary, had a traumatic sexual experience with her uncle when she was 17. Years later, when she was 26, that same uncle caused an even more traumatic experience, one that was not only painful, but caused Miriam to feel ashamed. Rape and molestation carries serious layers of pain, but for Miriam her physical response during that experience made her despondent. It took a sexual abuse counselor to explain that some women actually have an orgasm or similar response to a sexual act which happens against their will. This is a body's natural response, not one that signaled pleasure or consent.

For years she pushed the experience, (which happened within the "safety" of her home), to the back of her mind by pretending that it never happened. Then one day, out of the blue, Miriam received a call from her aunt requesting that she obtain a legal document for that same uncle. Out of respect for her aunt, Miriam complied. Days later she received a call from that uncle to thank her. Before Miriam could get him off the phone, he said, that he remembered what had happened in her house, and he'd been having wonderful dreams about it.

The feelings of shame welled up inside her as the memories came back to her in full force. Why did it feel so vivid and real and so hurtful all over again? especially since she had gone through so many spiritual transformations; many of which promised to clear away old past hurts and revitalize the body, mind, and spirit.

Suggestion:

I pointed out to Miriam that just like a Vietnam veteran who experiences the phantom itch or pain of a missing limb, when the body is traumatized, it remembers every detail. So does our emotional self. Miriam, decided to go on a spiritual and physical "cleansing." For a five week period, her food intake consisted mostly of raw fruits, vegetables, vitamins and minerals. Unaware of exactly what type of changes the cleansing would bring, Miriam experienced the effects on a multitude of levels. So as Miriam did a cleanse for her physical body for health, she was also subconsciously cleansing her emotional reserves of painful experiences.

Whatever we're holding onto must be cleaned out. A true spiritual cleansing is just like using Drano in our systems, it doesn't take out some of the hair; it takes out all of the hair. Once we start the process, we can't just say I only want it to happen this way. You can't expect the "Drano" to only clean some of the pipe, it sweeps through the entire pipe churning and foaming until it reaches the septic tank, and washes everything out and into the ocean.

Melanie now has another awareness of what took place during her cleansing and is grateful that she is on the road to becoming whole. Even though she still has flashbacks, she is to able to deal with them from a different perspective and seek the additional counseling that she needs from group therapy.

Case Study:

Another one of my life-coaching client is Samantha. She is very smart when it comes to her 9-to-5 five job. But when it comes to relationships, Samantha doesn't have a clue. For some reason she has a propensity to throw out all common sense when it comes to men.

Samantha, a 29-year old computer technician seemed to only engage in relationships with men who put extreme limits on their involvement with her. They only visit her at night, at strange hours, never wine or dine her—and never commit to a relationship with her. Samantha, somewhat overweight, and feeling a little less attractive for it, accepted that this was the only type of relationship she would have.

Upon further reflection and conversations with Samantha, I found that she had a strict, religious parent, then endured several years of strict (self-imposed) religious doctrines. Her last religious excursion led her into the next relationship with someone she nicknamed, "the back door man" (in the back door, a little take-out sex—and back out the door).

She finally found the strength to break it off with the man, and a few years later a girlfriend set her up with a blind date. Guess whom? To her amazement, the "back door man" made an unexpected reappearance back into her life. Against her better judgment, she started dating him again. Evidently the two of them weren't finished doing the *dating dance*. Their physical attraction was that strong, that another person was able to be conduit for the Universe and reunite the two.

Suggestion:

I asked her, "When did you say yes to this treatment? Just look at your life, you've traded one tightly controlling situation/person for another, then another. You were mentally conditioned for this type of relationship. Release it, put a period on it and put and end to it once and for all.

If you can't see a way to discontinue the restrictive limited relationship, then see it as a learning experience. Start looking for ways that you can say, "yes," I know this going to happen because it happened before and I'm going to chose a different route. Become somewhat of a detective in your relationships and act as if you are collecting data for someone else. We always have advice to give to other people, don't we? Once you remove your conscious mind from the day-to-day emotions of wanting and needing a crutch, (also know as a codependency), you will become aware of how this person was in your life to fulfill a need or to take you to the next level in life. Others would say that the person was there to teach you that lesson.

The people (and relationships) that come into our lives bring us all kinds of experiences. Some bring joy, love or happiness. Others bring tears or pain. Some even bring spiritual gifts that can help you find the true you.

When I speak of spiritual gifts, it may be an "unknown." It may not be evident to you at the time, but one day you have one of those "light bulb" moments where you say *damn!* (excuse my English, but you understand exactly the type of moments I mean) Maybe after six-to-seven months this person may be ready to move on.

Some relationships are just that—a great big learning experience, and no more than that. We tend to hold onto things longer than we should, and longer than our spiritual well-being will deem necessary. Some would call this a *need to be needed* regardless of the outcome. It is as though you have mistakenly won an Oscar and you are not going to give it back to the academy. But just like a production, how can one believe they can carry a whole movie without co-stars? Although, life is not a play nor is it a movie, but to some extent you must be able to share the spotlight with those around you. There is no need to step out of the light but there is a need to give and support. What I'm saying is that in relationships there will always be a *star* and *co-stars* but the gist of it all is that as long as you know the show must end, make it the best that you can and move on to the next without regret.

Here's how you can do that: first allow yourself to audition for different rolls (what people commonly know as dating), then allow yourself to be treated as if they couldn't make the movie without you (setting up your boundaries allowing a little give and take). Then next allow your co-star to read you their script, and if you like what you hear, then repeat your lines again to see if both are in sync. Now understand that this movie/play/relationship is good as long as the lead honors each other's craft, expertise, and ability. You must feel good about what you are experiencing and know that your supporting cast is just that, and I'll call them friends, family, and others. While you are doing this movie, play; learn everything you can about what goes into a good movie. Is it the lighting, the directing, the costumes? What I'm really saying is: stay in the moment when you are in a relationship and don't wonder what it would be like if you were with some other star. Stay in the moment by becoming aware of yourself, see what you can learn about you. That is the most important thing I can tell about relationships is learn all you can about you. It is not about the other person. It is *never* about the other person. It is always about how you feel about you and how you react to outside stimuli.

JOURNALING

Articulate in words:

1. What is the one thing you do to express self-love?

___

___

___

2. What ways do you show that you are an independent thinker? Explain.

___

___

___

3. What is the most important lesson you have learned in your relationships? Explain.

___

___

___

Chapter 14
Loneliness/Aloneness:

There are several definitions for the state of being lonely: solitary, desolate, dejected and saddened. This should not be confused with being alone, which is simply being by oneself, apart from anyone or anything.

Aloneness is more expansive than just being alone, it is akin to being in *silence*. It's being still with one's self for any given time.

Case Study:

I don't know if I should call Benjamin a client, for we are also friends. When Benjamin asked me to render my Life Coaching services to him, I had to consider the downside. Would I really tell him the truth? Or would I allow Benjamin to "slide" and not give his best? How would I go about challenging him to do the necessary assignments in the allotted time?

Benjamin stated on many occasions that he hates being at home alone. And that fear has kept him from moving forward in several aspects of his life. He says that he would prefer having someone to talk with while he is at home working, or just watching television. This amazed me because, from the outside looking in, anyone would think he was a well-rounded guy who did not need outside stimulation to complete his day. (Again another case of perception, looking at what the person is projecting and not at what they really feel). How did I not see it in his eyes? Did I overlook something in the handshake when we agreed to proceed with the coaching? What flags did I let slide in order to continue with the friendship?

Suggestion:

We all, to some degree, have times when we don't like ourselves and don't want to be alone with ourselves. Times when we seek out whimsical companionship or frivolous entertainment in an attempt to keep ourselves from dealing with the issue at hand. It is a though we know, deep down inside, that if we are alone we will be forced to deal with the true self. The self that we don't show to the outside world for fear someone will see the scars.

So the need to become whole and find that sense of true self is totally pushed aside. We move from one relationship to the next, rather than focusing on our inner self or developing a higher consciousness. Fear can be a blinding factor, allowing us to remain in relationships that are debilitating. Fear carries into our business ventures or personal projects, stifling our goals and dreams. We then become dissatisfied with the course of our lives, and are unable to identify the root cause. Fear, in most cases, is the culprit. Remove the fear and obstacles drop away from us like leaves from a tree. Remove the fear and when our intended soul mates appear, we recognize and appreciate them as such, and not just another "place holder" we hold onto until a "real number" comes along. Fear will make you settle for less than you deserve, creating a cycle of one step forward, one step back. Our lives become a constant two-step. Have you been doing your own brand of relationship two-step?

Break the cycle! Be true to yourself. Take a "Time Out." Use the time alone for clarity, meditation, focus; and for reflecting. Being alone does not mean that people don't love you or want to be around you. "Aloneness is not loneliness"; it is the time given to you to work on your desires, dreams and goals, without cumbersome noise and static.

When you take time for yourself and your goals, momentum is gained and you move forward, attracting experiences and people. You will be rewarded further with people who have the same goals, dreams and ideas. There will never be a time when you are alone that you won't have a great idea or thought.

"Being alone is the greatest gift you can give yourself."

This is truly a time to reassess your projects, it's a time to write, a time to think and a time to renew *you*.

How many times have you seen people glowing? And you wondered why? Is it because they have a spouse, significant other or someone who is winding them up every morning and sending them out into the world? Or is it because they are aware of who they are and have their own agenda in life?

Most of you would say, well that's nice, but I work hard, so at the end of the day it would be good to have someone to share my life with. This is a typical reaction to: *I don't like being alone.*

Think about how much richer that conversation would be if you were renewed within yourself? Wouldn't that conversation be just that much more interesting if you took some time alone to replay the events of the day in your head to make sure you were not bringing any negativity into a light-hearted atmosphere? Sure, being alone is quiet, but it is such a good time to regroup and do the things you really never get a chance to do. Have you ever stopped and asked yourself, what am I doing? Where am I going? Why am I in this car, shopping mall, bar, or health club? What are you running from? Most of time you are running from *yourself.*

When dealing with some clients, I'll dig a little deeper and find that they really don't like their own company. Is this another case of self-hate? Is this another case of "why me" syndrome? If that is the case, maybe seeing a professional counselor would be a good place to start. But if this is just a part of Life 101 that was not discussed with you, or you just happened to miss it, continue reading.

Okay, you say, I'm going to try this "Time Out" thing. Spend time alone. How do I go about doing that? First, allow yourself at least thirty minutes a day to be alone. During this time don't answer the phone (unless it's a true emergency—and I'm not talking about the what others *believe* to be an emergency). Maybe play some soft music, something that will play in the background and not affect the flow or your thoughts. During this time alone, eat healthy foods, take a bath, or lay on the sofa, and be ***free.***

At the end of that time say to yourself, "this was great, I can't wait for tomorrow." With all this renewed energy you can now place all the calls you want. If you choose go jump in your car and throw caution to the wind, you made it through the hour of being alone (but not lonely).

By repeating this ritual every day for the next few days, you will begin to be able to hold your own. You will gain strength to use against the forces that would have you leaving your home and driving aimlessly around town looking for outside stimuli. From this thirty minutes build to one, and then more. And before you know it you will be able to spend as much time by yourself as you need to finish off all those projects that never seem to get done. Keep in mind: being in neutral is just as effective and rewarding as being in drive.

JOURNALING

Articulate in words:

1. Do you enjoy your of own company? Explain.

____

____

____

2. Have you ever taken yourself to lunch?
   If not, why?

____

____

____

3. How would you spend an hour by yourself?
   Explain.

____

____

____

...Open your mind to anything that stimulates it and then digest it.

If what you want is cleared through your soul then you will not have to ask that question.

Chapter 15
Visualization

Visualization is seeing what you want in your mind. Think of it as the imagine-making power of the mind. To perceiving your desire in material form although it is still just a mental image. Visualization is actually ***acting as if*** you already have the desire or goal. Visualization is very big among "*thinkers*" from all walks of life. From Thomas Edison to Bill Gates, they all visualized what they wanted to happen in great detail. Visualization does not take a lot of time, nor does it take great deal of effort or any money.

Suggestion:

When visualizing, you need to hold in your mind what it is you want, as though it already existed. If it is a house that you desire, then you must see the house as though it was yours. You must decorate the house as if you lived in it. You must see the grass growing; you must hold the vivid image of shiny new floors made of rich cherry-wood. You must feel the texture of the wall paint, and smell the logs burning in the fireplace. You must see and feel it in your mind as though you owned that house and it was your home.

Visualization became the "hot new thing" in the 1980's and has been called everything from conceptual to creative. But it's all still visualization. And every aspect of it is within your reach.

JOURNALING

Articulate in words:

1. Have you ever used visualization in seeking your goals and desires? Explain.

____

____

____

2. Close your eyes. Now describe everything in your bedroom, think about it, then write it down. Now imagine, in the same space, a more luxurious suite expanding your outcome by using a visualization technique. Compare your results.

____

____

____

____

____

____

3. Then try this in other aspects of your life—small or larger desires. What were the results.

____

____

____

CHAPTER 16
MEDITATION

So should I meditate, visualize or use affirmations?

Let's break down the differences between them first. Meditation and visualization are both excellent forms of focusing the mind. Affirmation on the other hand is stating or repeating a short phrase over and over again until it becomes true. Unlike visualization, the mental imaging exercise, which I spoke about in the last chapter. Now let's look at meditation. **Meditation** is allowing the mind to be free of controlled thought, in a state of comptemplation. Also meditation is the act of daydreaming, being in an inwardly state and to ponder, reflect, or to speculate. Most people believe that when they meditate, the mind has to be free of all thought. That is not the case. Seemingly random thoughts will enter and exit the mind. The only thing you need to do is concentrate on your breathing and allow the flow to take you to a place of bliss. By flow, I mean allowing the Universe or higher consciousness to act on the body of thoughts that enter your mind and interact with you.

Suggestion:

There are many different meditation techniques, and just as many, if not more, books written on the subject. I would suggest perusing the meditation section of a New Age bookstore to find one that covers a style of meditation that suits you and your lifestyle. So make the time to rest your mind. Maybe start with fifteen minutes and gradually build to an hour. I usually do about a half hour. For some that is a lot and then there are others who would say that I'm just warming up. But I have found that just by sitting at my desk and closing my eyes and taking deep, long breaths for a short period of time helps to put me in a meditative state. It's a good tool for regaining your center. You can also sit in your car and meditate before you go into that next meeting or mall and find peace of mind. When you are doing this exercise, allow yourself to become centered so you can refocus your energy.

It is very important that you find your center. One way to find your center is to ask your higher self or consciousness, *what is it that I should know today?* Then proceed to ask the questions you need to have answered. Your higher self and Source energy are there waiting to help you. There is no way you can be in control of your life if you do not become one with the Source. You may have good intentions, but intentions are nothing with without a base. So meditation can be a great tool to help you find your center. Meditation is a very important part in achieving harmony with yourself and your desire.

JOURNALING

Articulate in words:

1. Have you ever meditated before? If not why?

___

___

___

2. What are some of the advantages of meditating? explain

___

___

___

CHAPTER 17
ENJOY THE JOURNEY

Ahhh, and now for the Journey. What is a journey you say, well the dictionaries defined it as; an excursion, usually a brief tour or trip for pleasure, health, etc. a journey on important business or for self-gratification; the act of traveling from one place to another, it's an itinerary, a junket, a march, an odyssey and an adventure. Now with that said, let's begin our Journey.

As you enjoy your journey through life, with your map in hand and tool pouch strapped to your side it may help you to remember that if you **promise** yourself the riches of the Universe, they will be yours.

We are magical beings able to magnificently create whatever life we deem satisfactory. I have listened to so many people talking about someone promising them Utopia and then not following through. The anger that I detected, directed at that person for breaking that promise was so strong and the emotions are so overwhelming. You would think that the offending person was in absolute control of the other's well-being. In order to move forward in life, you must make a promise to *yourself*. You must look at your life from the perspective that, "No one can bestow upon you anything that you don't give yourself."

Whether that is giving yourself love, encouragement or the right to have fun, it all comes down to "what do you want?"

There have been numerous scholars and great teachers of New Age wisdom that state: the first step toward being successful and achieving your desires and goals, is *knowing what you want*. Once you know what you want, only then can you stop talking about what you do not want.

The second step, of course, would be to create a plan of action. This plan needs to describe how you are going to get to your destination, and what will be your outcome. I know you would like to believe that there is some outside source calling all the shots in your life, but that cannot be. We are all given choices, and the power to *think*. How and when we use that power is reflected in our lives. You have the ability to control your destiny and live your desires. But it takes focus to plan a glorious outcome, to visualize, meditate, and just gaze upon what you desire. We create our own reality minute by minute, whether or not we think we do. Our "thoughts" play such a prominent role in our everyday lives. They are living creatures, waiting to be nurtured with energy and emotions.

Almost every aspect of our lives can be traced back to some "thought." Every thought vying to be the dominate one. As each thought jockeys for position, you walk through life wondering if you should love or hate, act or react, or make a choice. Whether you call it creative chaos or call them blessings, these thoughts, be they new or forgotten ones, start to cling to each other and build a platform from which you spout your truths. **It is through thinking that man forms that which he has in life. (Proverbs 23:7)** As you continue your quest for that which you are seeking, keep in mind that you are in total control of how you feel at any given moment in time. No one can affect your attitude but you. How we see ourselves and what we reflect back to others is what we have grown to believe about ourselves. Yet we always have the free will to change our "thoughts" in order to change our lives and reach our goals and desires. By applying affirmations, visualization, meditation or even gazing, you can start to achieve your goals.

As I stated earlier in this book, affirmations can be pictures writings, recordings, songs or the spoken word. The real idea behind it all is to *feel the words*. ***"Act As If"*** until it becomes a natural part of who you are. Intentions are great, but by knowing what you want, you can truly be free. Freeing yourself is freeing your mind of the shackles that you cannot see, but which hold you in a place of stuck. And if you are still feeling "stuck," stop and ask yourself: "what is it that I want." Then you will get more insight and clarity.

I've always lived by the mantra that if you desired anything, you had to *speak it into existence*. This science of life is called **the Law of Attraction,** that which is likened to itself will be drawn to it. Like begets like. (Luke 12:32).

So see it in your mind, ***act as if*** *you* already have it, own it, or posses it, and prepare for it. Make room in your heart, soul, mind, and environment, so that it may flow freely to you. All these criteria must be met before you can receive it. But even with these tools, you still need a written plan of action, and possibly support from your friends and family members to keep you on your path. For on one hand are all the riches of the Universe waiting for you, but on the other, self-sabotage. I say *self* because no one can create more madness in your life than your own inner demons — your old beliefs.

It's all about becoming aware of what you desire and staying focused. Allowing yourself to become wholly immersed in the Universe, using your imagination and visualization to create the life you desire. Completely becoming one with your higher self. Creating a center from which to receive guidance from a higher source. Being able to see yourself in the past, and understanding that choices you made which caused you some pain may have been for a higher learning experience. *All that matters is that you made it to today, still intact and able to seek further enlightenment.* All this comes with the understanding that you are living in the **NOW.**

There comes a time in everyone's life that they have to make a decision about what is their true heart's desire. You must realign your thinking, dream up new intentions and remember: no matter how many voices whisper that you cannot have it, do it, or be it, you must let your inner self and that subconscious mind of yours know that *everything is possible*. And yes, regardless of any situation, your thoughts will bring into existence, anything you can imagine is possible. As long as there is enough emotion and concentrated energy given to the object of your desire. How long will that take? You will see the object of your desire several times on your journey, appearing and reappearing as different situations strengthening your resolve to actually bring that desire to fruition. When you are vibrationally aligned with your desire, that is when you will receive all that you have dreamed about. I think you'll be surprised that what you were seeking was at the same time seeking you.

When you change your "thoughts" you can change your life. Effortlessly, you will begin to understand how you affect the people around you. Whether that is your boss, co-workers or family, your actions will have an affect on them. It's called bleed-through. It doesn't really matter if your intentions were to seek love, approval or attention from your family or friends, you must look within and find sustenance. Then allow yourself the right to be wrong, to take a fall, and just get back up and say I don't know, but I'm ready now and stronger.

"We may get one thing done, but there will always be more to do." No one person has all the right answers, not the Guru on the mountaintop, not the minister, not even the President. So you cannot get it wrong, it is just your perception of how you think others view that which you call your life. You can not serve the Source if you are not whole.

You cannot serve the Source if you are "broken." You cannot serve the Source if you are filled with hatred. You not serve the Source if your heart is filled with sorrow.

Breath only pure air, ask the Universe daily: "am I on my path." Always allow yourself to be free from any thing other than good. If you cannot feel good about what you are doing, then change course and allow your inner spirit to be the guide.

Give yourself room to grow without limiting yourself to other's ideas, find your own truth. How do you become unstuck? One Universal ***"dissolvent "*** which could be used, would be to become one with ***"All That Is."***

A physical ***"dissolvent"*** would be to stop thinking that what you are doing now is not good enough. Then continue to only think of yourself as if you have already achieved your desired goals and dreams. Let your life reflect your success. Let it be known that you have the key to achieving any goal or desire. Let it be said that you can not be anything other than that, which you seek.

Let it be known that you will only speak about that which you are. What I am saying is to become one with who you say you are, will only create a perfect—spiritually connected, Universal seeking, highly-enlightened, desire having, goal achieving, at peace with yourself -person. We all came here to experience the fruits of the Universe.

We probably will not achieve the fulfillment of all our desires because there will always be another one. And when you attain that desire, there will be yet another one waiting. So just enjoy the journey and allow everyone else the space to find their path. Even if we don't like what we see on that other person's path, it is not up to us to judge. And for that matter, no one should have the ability to affect our path with their judgments.

Knowing and embracing the Laws of the Universe have opened my heart, my mind and my eyes.

"Universal Blessings" to all that I have met on my path who were gracious enough to share their love with "No Hidden Agendas."

JOURNALING

1. What is your life's journey? Explain.

____

____

____

2. Is what you are doing now, helping to facilitate what you want? Explain.

____

____

____

3. What is on your path right now? How can it help you? (friends, family, education, job, etc.)

____

____

____

4. What is on your path right now, that you can change for the better? (i.e. clutter, baggage, disabling beliefs.) What steps will you take to make that change?

____

____

____

5. What would make your journey easier? Explain.

____

____

____

6. Do you really want to achieve your goals or desires? Explain.

____

____

____

7. What you would do with your goal and desire once you receive it?

____

____

____

8. How would your goals and desires change once you achieved them? How would it affect your attitude, outlook on life, etc. Explain.

____

____

____

9. Picture yourself as already achieving your goals and desires. What do they feel like. Explain.

____

____

____

10. Are you living in accordance with the laws of the Universe? Explain.

____

____

____

LET'S PRETEND

11. Now ask yourself, "If I could take a radical sabbatical and live the life I have dreamed of . . ." Think--what would that be?

____

____

____

12. Then why aren't you living that dream now?

____

____

____

13. What resources do you need to start?

____

____

____

14. Now let's pretend someone gave you all those resources. What continues to keep you from moving toward you dreams, goals and desires?

____

____

____

Let's Get Real

Journaling

Articulate in words:

1. Where do you see yourself twenty years from now? Explain.

____

____

____

2. When you look back twenty years from now, can you say what you are doing at this moment in time was beneficial to your long-term life plan. Explain?

____

____

____

3. What is your long-range plan?

____

____

____

[Do you plan on working at a superstore twenty years from now, greeting customers with a nervous twitch in one eye caused by years of stress, anguished and uncompleted desires and goals?] Then you should ask yourself why you didn't take care of business when the opportunity was given. Carpe Diem! Sieze the day.

You will know what you want when what you are doing runs out.

Time is only there to allow you to see what you have done in the past.

It isn't how much you know, but what you do with what you do know.

Open the door, walk through it and free yourself. But unlock it first . . .

.Your ego is not you, but it's a good place to start the search for you!

.

.From where you stand can you see you?

Take time to walk with the you, the person you don't know.

Love is only the beginning, now comes the demonstration.

Certificate of Success

May it be known that this Certificate has been presented to

____

For Outstanding Achievement in attaining Their Life's Dreams, Goals and Desires

Presented Proudly This Day by Ehrych F. Gilmore, CH

EPILOGUE

When I was writing this book, I was still trying to figure out how I glossed over and not delved deeper into these issues. The issues of parental relationships, other personal relationships and most importantly sex, especially when subjects of this nature are so relevant to deeper issues of seeking approval from family and others. These topics were very intriguing to me, but I didn't think enough people would want to read about them in the context of ***"WHY AM I STUCK?"***.

In the beginning, I couldn't see how these issues related to, or affected so many of my Life Coaching clients, when they were coming to me under the pretext of career related coaching. I started to wonder "Was I running away from these issues or had I actually incorporated them, these different experiences into my life, to fit neatly with who I am?"

So let's talk a little bit about these unresolved issues of relationships, sex, and family. You may have experienced some of these issues in your own personal life. Who really examines these unresolved issues beyond *"I want what I want, and you are stopping me from having my desire?"* I have found that in most cases whether it is with your mother, father, friends or significant other, it's easier to point the finger of blame, shame or guilt than to deal with them straight-on.

Who would ever admit to disliking anything about their mother? It goes against everything we are taught, Mom, apple pie or peach cobbler, **"GOD"** and country. To bear ones dirty laundry...it just doesn't happen unless you are seeing a *"shrink"*, or telling your Life Coach what's really at the bottom of this situation you now find yourself confronted with.

To dislike how you related to your father is not hard. He represented the strong root, the foundation of the family in my house. You knew the answer to any question was ***No!*** *Can I go?* ***No!****, Can I have?* ***No!***. It just didn't matter what the situation or question, the only answer was ***No!***... but that was for you own good (*hmmm*).

We invite into our lives what we think about, and who is not carrying around old baggage (i.e., old negative thoughts)? Baggage that just keep growing and growing and growing because we want to prove that our parents were not right about their assessments of life. It's almost like we want to pay back the grief for not being able to have our own independent ideas.
If you look carefully and examine why occurrences in your current relationship seem like de j'vue, it is probably because you have married or are dating your father or mother, figuratively speaking. Take time and examine your relationship from breakfast to the bed,

if you know what I mean. As you sort through these issues of sex, marriage and career, you're probably still trying to resolve all this impeachable data, that was handed down and now stored in your subconscious mind. You ***can*** mentally release yourself from all of those *"no you can't"*, *"do as I say"*, and *"do as your told"* anchors. When you quiet your mind and go within yourself, you'll see that you've probably been trying to figure out how to win *(the big payback)*, but that is not necessary anymore. You can now go inside of yourself and take a step in freeing yourself by saying, "Mother what I have not told you is that I now know when you were a little stressed with me, it was due to the resources you had at the time."

That's easy to say because it goes back to apple pie and motherhood. The father thing may be a little harder, because you're coming from a place of negative words that have anchored you. These anchors became the weight in the baggage carried into all of your everyday life situations. Check your daily routines to see if you can identify any of these anchors. In moving forward in your life you could say to your father, I love you for providing a home for me, and giving me structure. But that ***"No"*** will probably still have a bigger and a longer lasting effect in your mind, if you have not reprogrammed yourself to know that you do not need the approval of others.

What you have realized about your relationships with your parents may be, they were working from their core beliefs, or maybe from another source of beliefs, and what was in their resource toolbox of life at the time. Whether it was societal or generational, this is what made your parents who they were then and are today.

Expanding on the principles of Universal Law, they are always working. It is how we choose to make them work with us or against us that gives them manifestation in your life. The choice is yours. Using affirmations like "*I am great*", "*I am a great person*", "*I'm a great lover, friend, spouse*", etc. don't matter if you don't believe it, or if you don't practice it. In dealing with any of life's issues, you have to know you are, what you think you are. In others words,
"So as a man thinketh he is".

Now, how do you go about getting started to create your goals, dreams, and desires? ***First***, I would suggest that you write down all your goals and desires. ***Second***, I would suggest that you pick one goal to which you feel you can commit yourself, regardless of any obstacles and follow the steps outlined in page 112 . ***Third***, still there are other ways in which you can kind of get your feet wet before committing wholeheartedly.

You could join clubs, associations, or just old fashion networking activities, whether on a large or small scale, with people you want to emulate. Also, you can study, read or watch T.V. on subjects that are related to your desires and goals. Start small and build to larger projects. It's like always finding that special parking space, use that as a gauge. Say to yourself *"If I can create this parking space each and every time, I can create my desire."* **Fourth**, you can support yourself, your spouse, friends or significant other in reaching each other's goals, dreams and desires by thinking, "How can I make this situation better?" One way would be to call your support partner during the day, checking to make sure if you are following the goals you agreed to work on for the day.

Also, shopping at specialty bookstores and picking up the latest on any books, tapes, or CD's that might add to the resources that are needed. Another way would be to leave a voice message of encouragement to yourself or significant other during the day. Attend one day or weekend seminars, check the local papers for outreach centers or the library for upcoming events. As you do, for others during the day do the same thing for yourself.

So when you speak and say I am... say it as if you can not change it!

Simple Steps to attain your goals, dreams and desires:

1. You must be specific about what you want.

2. You must identify what you want (*who, what, where, when, and how*), and how it will make you feel to have it!

3. You must see everything you want as if it already exists in your life. ***"Act As If"*** Open your mind to receive in the ***"Now"***

4. You must write down what you want, to the completion of what it smells, tastes, sounds, and feels like. ***Visualize it until it materializes.*** It must be excepted by the mind as attainable.

5. You must enjoy the journey of attaining the desire, dream, or goals as if they were in material form already.

6. You must have a plan:
   You will need a blueprint with deadlines of when you plan to achieve your goal.

7. You must work your plan:
You must devote time working your plan. You must post pictures or charts to view and check everyday to evaluate where you are in accordance to your plans of achieving you goals and desires.

8. You must capitalize on both internal and external resources that you are going to need to achieve these desires (*time, books, space, workshops or partnership, etc.*).

9. Listen to motivational tapes and CDs, or read about other positive people that have achieved the success or desires, that you are working toward.

10. Stay focused when obstacles arise and remember it's your ***thoughts*** that will control any situation. Keep in mind what is the end result.

What is your end result?

"I now know my name, it is Invisible"

RECOMMENDED READING

Before You Think Another Thought by Bruce Doyle

Ask and It Is Given: Learning to Manifest Your Desires by Jerry and Esther Hicks

How to Change Your Life by Ernest Holmes

Empowerment: The Art of Creating Your Life as You Want it by David Gershon and Gail Straub

Speak it into Existence by Sesvalah, LCSW and Naleighna Kai

You Can Heal Your Life by Louise L. Hay

30-Day Mental Diet by Willis Kinnear

Your Life: Why it is the Way it is and What You Can Do About it by Bruce McArthur

The Basic Principles of the Science of the Mind by Dr. Frederick Bailes

It Works if You Work it! by Johnnie Coleman, D. D. D.H.L.

Note: All internal quotes are attributed to Ehryck F. Gilmore, CH

Ehryck F. Gilmore, CH is a Certified Hypnotherapist, Life Coach, Reiki Practitioner, Empowerment Coach and Intuitive Counselor. He has studied at the Omega Center in Rhinebeck, New York, attended DePaul University, Moody Bible Institute and the School of Spiritual Psychology of Milwaukee. He is also a master practitioner of Neuro-Linguistic Programming and studied at the NLP Institute of Chicago.

Today, Ehryck F. Gilmore, CH, lists author and consultant among his credentials, with his new book: Why Am I Stuck? The Science of Releasing Yourself from Being Held A Mental Hostage, Through his Consultancy and the No Hidden Agenda's Seminars, he has helped clients, some from as far as London, UK and Ireland, achieve success on professional and personal levels with personal consulting, nationwide seminars and workshops. Ehryck resides in the Metropolitan Chicago area and is currently working on his next book, "No Hidden Agenda's" entitled after his seminars, and is planning a national tour in 2005.

Visit him on the web:
www.ehryckgilmore.com.